AI and Ed

AI and Ed

Education in an Era of Artificial Intelligence

George A. Goens

ROWMAN & LITTLEFIELD
Lanham • Boulder • New York • London

Published by Rowman & Littlefield
An imprint of The Rowman & Littlefield Publishing Group, Inc.
4501 Forbes Boulevard, Suite 200, Lanham, Maryland 20706
www.rowman.com

6 Tinworth Street, London, SE11 5AL, United Kingdom

British Library Cataloguing in Publication Information Available

Library of Congress Cataloging-in-Publication Data

Names: Goens, George A., author.
Title: Ai and ed : education in an era of artificial intelligence / George
    A. Goens.
Other titles: Artificial intelligence and education
Description: Lanham : Rowman & Littlefield, [2021] | Includes
    bibliographical references and index. | Summary: "The purpose of
    this book is to define the role of education and its goals, content, and
    approaches that will assist citizens in addressing the challenges the
    artificial intelligence movement brings to daily life of citizens"—Provided
    by publisher.
Identifiers: LCCN 2021024315 (print) | LCCN 2021024316 (ebook) |
    ISBN 9781475858266 (Cloth : acid-free paper) | ISBN 9781475858273
    (Paperback : acid-free paper) | ISBN 9781475858280 (ePub)
Subjects: LCSH: Artificial intelligence—Educational applications.
Classification: LCC LB1028.43 .G64 2021 (print) | LCC LB1028.43 (ebook)
    | DDC 371.33/4—dc23
LC record available at https://lccn.loc.gov/2021024315
LC ebook record available at https://lccn.loc.gov/2021024316

♾™ The paper used in this publication meets the minimum requirements of American
National Standard for Information Sciences—Permanence of Paper for Printed Library
Materials, ANSI/NISO Z39.48-1992.

For
Marilyn

Contents

Chapter 1

Transformation

Just when the caterpillar thought the world was over, it became a butterfly.

—English proverb

We delight in the beauty of a butterfly, but rarely admit the changes it has gone through to achieve that beauty.

—Maya Angelo

Butterflies have always been a beautiful and intriguing symbol of dramatic change and metamorphosis. They evolve from eggs to caterpillars to butterflies, and live, depending on the species, one to nine months. Their journey is a symbol of beauty, growth, and transformation: signifying that small changes can create dramatic alterations in life. But what do butterflies have to do with people and society?

Mathematician and meteorologist Edward Lorenz, a founder of the concept of chaos theory, posed the question, "Does the flap of a butterfly's wings in Brazil set off a tornado in Texas?"[1] In essence, relatively small actions create dramatic effects. Chaos theory concerns the unpredictability of complex, nonlinear systems; for example, social, economic, political, and organizations. They do not always operate linearly or mechanically—"things" happen.

Lorenz illustrated that some complex dynamic systems exhibit unpredictable behavior in which small variances have a profound impact on conditions and outcomes. His view is contrary to Sir Isaac Newton's assertion that the universe operated like a linear mechanistic system like clockwork: predictable based on linear cause-and-effect relationships.

Perspectives about the world and life are formulated, in part, by perception and how people think. Linear thinkers perceive the world as a logical and rational system operating primarily in a black and white manner. To solve a problem or condition, a straight-line course of action is pursued. Set a goal and then define the sequential steps to get there. A response to each step is necessary to move on to the next: it is a strategy not open to nuance or emotion.

Linear thinking rests on methodic, analytic, and logical thinking. Making or not making a decision can have a large impact. Straight sequential steps are pursued consistently applying the best information and formulas. Linear analysis and strategic plans often fall short because of intangibles and subtleties that have deeper impact than logic would indicate.

The present environment is not fixed in stone, change is inevitable, and in many ways essential. A dynamic environment is not always predictable: consequently, planning and strategic linear steps may not be effective. People live in a world of unpredictable events, circumstances, and a bit of randomness.

Linear thinking presupposes that elements operate sequentially and predictably. Strategic planning is an example of linear thinking: consecutive steps operating in sequence and actions are defined to reach a goal or solve a problem. Many business and social enterprises strategically plan moving step-by-step and part-to-part.

However, the phrase "the best-laid plans of mice and men often go awry" is indicative of the failure of linear plans for unanticipated reasons. People do not realize that social or economic systems are chaotic and do not always move in logical and expected sequences. Sometimes a slight modification brings consequential change.

Logic is based on reasoning and dedication to the validity of rational thought. The problem is the world does not always work in a logical and rational pattern. Butterflies exist in nature and human events. Logic does not always explain conditions or human behavior, particularly concerning emotional or crisis circumstances. While a plan may be strategically valid, reason is often diverted by emotion, intuition, or relatively minor events.

Individuals negate other approaches as options because of their established mindset. Inflexibility in perception and thinking can result in a lack of options and progress. How people think is often the basis for how they comprehend issues and solutions.

Society and the environment are complex, interconnected open systems. Nonlinear thinkers use spiral thinking and problem solving, which opens multiple directions and starting points to address issues or problems. They examine events to determine the root cause because there are levels and layers of possible concerns and influences. Events are the result of multiple causation and the cognitive and emotional relationships between people, forces, and events.

Nonlinear thinkers make connections and apply conclusions from unrelated perspectives: they do not always work sequentially. Creativity and intuition are applied, resulting in multiple possibilities and directions. Complex thinking is necessary in chaotic social or scientific circumstances. Discussion, debate, and diversity of thought are required to identify new patterns and to self-organize.

Many leaders propose changes to systems and structures to address contemporary circumstances. However, just changing them can be futile unless the thinking that created them is altered, particularly when transformations are evident. Paradigms and change require independent thinking. As philosopher Friedrich Nietzsche stated, "Even a thought, even a possibility can shatter and transform us."

Historically, the "butterfly effect" has been at work. In fact, it may not follow a reasoned or probable sequence. The stock market is a chaotic system that continually revamps over time influenced by unforeseen and unplanned events. The fluctuation in the market is dependent on attitudes, actions, and events, some of which could not be forecasted. Attitudes and fear arise and the market reacts, sometimes minimally, and at other times with deep repercussions. Forecasting and planning become the victims of intangibles and unexpected butterflies.

Politics and history hold examples of minor events or occurrences creating significant events or developments. It could be argued that a piece of masking tape, for example, led to the impeachment of a president. A Watergate building security guard discovered that a door with two locks had been taped open with masking tape. At first, he thought employees placed the tape there for the ease of entry so as not to have to continually use a key to enter. He removed the tape. But then the guard discovered the door had been re-taped, and he became suspicious and called the authorities. As a result, the historic Watergate scandal unfolded with the demise of a president as the outcome.

Change materializes in a number of ways—some planned and others a result of "butterflies." The recent pandemic is an example that closed down social, economic, and political systems. A single dramatic or expected event did not start the pandemic: it evolved and progressed in individual increments over a relatively short period of time and affected a great share of the world's population. The result altered work, businesses, personal connections, professional relationships, and economic and societal structures.

Planning, in other words, cannot assume stability and a guaranteed process and outcomes. According to Henry Mintzberg, "Planning is fundamentally a conservative process: it acts to conserve the basic orientation of the organization, specifically its existing categories. Thus, planning may promote change in the organization, but of a particular kind: change within the context of the organization's overall orientation; change at best in strategic positions within the overall strategic perspective. Expressed differently, in our view planning works best when the broad outlines of the strategy are already in place, not when significant strategic change is required from the process itself."[2] At times, plans had to be made as the circumstances involved, because the situation evolved very quickly. While emergency plans are available, they may not address the specific crisis at hand.

However, in times of transformation, significant change usually is expected and required. Some situations bring expected major changes. The machine, for example, altered life dramatically in almost all sectors of life. The gas engine created a revolution in travel, roads, corporations, and social networks. Technology, another obvious example, transformed many aspects of life, and continues to do so. Innovations and renovations do not happen overnight but reforms continue to broaden their impact through refinement and creativity and the development of other supportive inventions or discoveries.

CHANGE AND TRANSFORMATION

Change and transformation are not synonymous. While many apply these terms interchangeably, there is a clear distinction. Change is not necessarily a transformation, however, transformation involves change.

Change can be small and incremental refinements to present circumstances, strategies, or products: modifying, substituting, or replacing something. Change management in organizations means defining and enacting specific, finite, and planned modifications. Innovations in major systems are geared to produce more proficient and productive ways of completing current undertakings and getting better results. Business and manufacturing rely on innovation to produce new and established products and outcomes more efficiently and cost-effectively.

Transformation on the other hand moves far beyond shifts in approaches or methods. Making changes is far easier than transforming a system or organization. In a sense, transformation creates a new reality. The scope is larger and focused on altering or modifying beliefs because beliefs affect thinking, and thinking affects goals, values, actions, and behavior. "The overall goal of transformation is not just to execute a defined change, but to reinvent the organization and discover a new or revised business model based on the vision of the future."[3] Transformation entails a much greater risk and is more unpredictable because the impact of a failure is far more precarious than remaining static.

Transformation alters the essence of organizations and individuals. "Change fixes the past. Transformation creates the future."[4] Change is directed at fixing and improving, whereas transformation is geared to creating and designing the future and inventing ways to achieve it.

According to Irvine Laszlo, "This is an era of *macroshift*: a shift that is all-embracing, rapid, and irreversible, extending to the far corners of the globe and involving practically all aspects of life. It is driven by technology, but the stresses and conflicts it creates do not have purely technological solutions."[5] Macroshifts affect all aspects of society including examining values and principles, and the impact on the evolution of traditional systems.

Transformation modifies beliefs and strategies to examine the future through a mindset that brings conversion and renovation to organizations or life. Thinking and developing a perspective on an unfolding future is more difficult and deeper than making the present more efficient. Efficiency does not matter if the need is irrelevant. For example, a more efficient telegraph is useless because of the transformation in electronics and satellites. Redefinition, at times, is necessary to survive in the future.

HISTORY

Obviously today, things are different than in decades past. Historically, the United States experienced many social and economic transformations in the last century. "The last decade of the 20th Century was *qualitatively* and *quantitatively* different not only from what they were in the first years of this (20th) century but also from what has existed at any other time in history: in their configurations, in their processes, in their problems, and in their structures."[6]

Some analysts indicate that change and transformation come in cycles or "waves" initiated by innovation. Often these innovations bring about commercial, industrial, and corporate reform. The United States experienced a number of these conversions due to industrial and technological advances that have benefits and profit in terms of services, products, or business operations. To do so requires a process of continuous examination of new ideas and the dynamics of change.

The cycles or waves of transformation in United States included[7] (* indicates it reached its peak):

- Financial—agricultural: 1600–1780
- Industrial revolution: 1780–1880
    - Steam engine textile manufacturing: 1817*
    - Railroads and steel making: 1870*
    - Electricity: 1920*
    - Automobiles and petrochemicals: 1975*
- Information technology: now

Obviously, the impact of innovation and science is a major factor in these periods. The times transform as new equipment, processes, and technology advance. New issues and problems arise because innovation has upsides and downsides. The automobile brought the ease of travel but also concerns for the environment and safety.

In the nineteenth century, farmers were prominent, but by the 1900s, the blue-collar worker and the manufacturing industry began to advance. The number of small farmers receded as this change took place. Blue-collar employees worked as machine operators and as industrialization grew the need for them expanded.

Industry became a stabilizing force socially and economically. Industrial workers combined systematic manual work with mechanized equipment. Farmers and domestic workers, who were reducing in numbers, moved into industrial jobs, which required no additional education beyond the skills they already had.

By the mid-century (1959), the United States transformed from an industrial society to one requiring "knowledge workers." These jobs demanded different skills and abilities than industrial work, making the transition to these roles much more difficult. Knowledge workers gained access to jobs via education and training because those careers required different skills and abilities than industrial employees. Specialized knowledge, autonomous work, and decision making require preparation and the ability to master specialized and technical fields.

Mechanical breakthroughs, coupled with the growth of industrialism, created a number of adjustments and social consequences. Industrialization caused people to relocate from their small towns and villages to big cities where factories were located. This move had obvious effects on politics and economics. In cities and large towns, people became less active in the community than in the small towns and communities they left.

As a consequence, bureaucracy grew to meet individual and community needs and to push for efficient programs. Bureaucracies were established to move to greater productivity, which in many cases had the opposite effect, and became seen as the antithesis of efficiency: filled with red tape and regulations.

In business and factories, scientific management excelled. Roles and requirements were specified, along with accountability procedures, which employees were expected to meet. The role-bound process meant that workers were just supposed to get specific tasks and work completed in a timely manner.

Simply, individuals had to follow the organizational processes—their individual values, beliefs, passions, relationships, and others were not considered. In a sense, this alienated people because they did not gain meaning from simply being a faceless worker in a bureaucracy continually and repeatedly completing a designated task or role. People did not really feel a part of the larger picture: they were just "cogs" in the wheel.

According to a PEW research study, the diminishing importance of physical skills in jobs is due to the decline in manufacturing. The manufacturing sector cut back jobs that required physical skills, reducing one-third of its workforce from 1992 to 2015.[8]

Applying theoretical and analytical knowledge and skills was necessary. College education took greater prominence because knowledge included skills and aptitudes to continue to learn and analyze data and information. Knowledge also includes highly developed precise manual skills, not just cognitive recall or analysis, for example, surgeons and airline pilots require both.

Applied knowledge—specialization—became more important. Technicians, computer specialists, and others in science, the arts, and astrophysics became more notable. Knowledge-intensive employment in areas of education, health, law, engineering, business, and others grew dramatically. The interaction of research, thinking, and analytic skills, as well as cultural understanding, grew because of the nature of science and social adjustments. Dramatic change in most aspects of life was becoming more evident.

Technology, communication innovations, and the Internet influenced employment, society, and productivity. Social changes were set in motion through historic legislation on human rights, and important Supreme Court decisions moved the nation closer to its ideals of equal opportunity, equity, freedom of speech, and other major principles.

Wisdom is very important in examining the philosophical implications of change and innovation and their implications for democracy and established principles and values. A fair and moral society and the operation of its systems are based on a foundation of values and ethics. Ethics and value-based judgments are important in a fast-changing society to ensure that it maintains adherence to basic principles and tenets. Issues arise: not all of them positive. Online concerns about civility, harassment, privacy, and truth exist today, and potentially continue even with innovation. Discerning truth from propaganda and falsehoods is more necessary today than ever before because communication is omniscient and from a variety of sources.

Autocratic regimes negate standards and principles. Basic values are destroyed in the interest of power, personal gain, or control. Transformation brings and raises new issues based on established moral values and ethics that direct decisions on implementation and operation. The concerns today about surveillance and privacy have emanated from the power of technology.

TYPES OF TRANSFORMATIONS

Everyone marvels at the changes they experienced over their lifetimes. Demographic changes and the numbers in each generational category affect employment and attitudes, for example, retirement of baby boomers and fewer births. Parents frequently use the phrase "when I was a kid . . ." to explain to children how different things were years ago in their youth. Retiring employees discuss the "old days," generally pointing out how today things were easier than in those "days." One so-called senior citizen remarked to his grandson that "back then, I remember talking to an operator if I wanted to make a telephone call."

Certainly grandparents express astonishment at how today's society, culture, and economy transformed during their lifetime in the move from a mechanical to a technological society. Relatives who were born during the Great Depression would say to their children, "If you don't want to work in a factory like me, then you better graduate from high school." Education was perceived almost solely as a means to find employment and get a "good job." The loss of industrial jobs and the application of technology to manufacturing and industry had an impact on many workers, as some jobs moved overseas because of competition.

Intangibles are very powerful in the acceptance or rejection of change because it is not always positive, as history has demonstrated. Pluses and minuses come with all because there is no panacea. Optimism and fear are often strong forces in determining peoples' perspective along with an individual's mindset. Perspective, in part, is formed from past experiences, values, and frame of mind. With time, individuals must examine their thinking and identify any "blind spots" through self-reflection and analysis because they affect perspective and judgment.

Transformations occur in many sectors. They are not isolated or independent from each other: the impact in one sector affects others. Transformations, for example, in technology dramatically altered communication in every facet of life. The universal impact of computer and other technology is dramatic and the impetus of major reforms in what, how, and where people work and live.

Social transformations affect values and perspectives. Society is a system of social relationships that change with time. Demographics, communication, employment patterns, and needs affect people in all dimensions of formal and informal relationships. Jobs are created and others eliminated: each generation has experienced some of these alterations and innovations.

Social structures influence relationships and how people or groups relate with each other. Interaction and communication transformed significantly compared to how it was done a generation or two before. The social issues over the past fifty years and the attitude and priorities socially and politically demonstrate dramatic renovation and impact. Instant communication is available at the touch of a phone or computer. People have easy electronic access to information, books, libraries, and universities for data and information.

Networks are common aspects of life. They concern connecting people together for information assistance. Technology is commonly assumed to be part of a network linking computers and other devices for communications and data.

With them, there also complications, some of which moved beyond technological life. To begin, social media was to "make the world more open and connected."[9] People assumed an increase in sharing and connecting will be good for democracy, but several issues have arisen.

Communication is supposed to include talking (writing) and listening (reading). Unfortunately passing judgment occurs in people's need to impress others and results in arrogance and grandstanding. Parsing judgment is prevalent, and includes misinformation, along with gossip and outrage.

Judgments are presented to garner self-esteem and make moral verdicts and criticize others for their lack of accepting their opinions—some of which are far from the truth.

Two components are a part of communication to include context and intent of the message. Often individuals distort the intent of a message and its context to provoke negative reactions. The intent is to provoke an immediate negative reaction. They do not take time to reflect: they just erupt.

Of course, today there is "fake news," which is intended to get people riled and react to the false information or political positions. Individuals galvanize at different ends of the philosophical or political position and do not listen to each other. They become outraged and name-call as well as categorize others in negative ways.

Free speech should help others listen and understand each other. Understanding why someone holds a position they do is critical and necessary. It may even move individuals to see into another person's life and why they hold the idea or concept that they do.

Connection is not synonymous with communication. Critical thinking can lead to deeper understanding and relationship. A nation of epithets is a nation headed for a destructive history.

Social movements may not be universally accepted. Innovation springs from creative interactions, as well as conflict, which sometimes move quickly and with considerable force. The nature of engagement about conditions and consequences, however, does not have to be negative, even though they may not be universally valued or totally understood.

Societal transformation raises hostility, as personal security and ambitions may be threatened. Rapid change can be destabilizing. Competition for power and position becomes vulnerable. The economy is one dimension of life that all people experience in all facets of their lives and the future. However, technology and the Internet have made uncertainty more prominent with repercussions in many aspects of life.

The COVID-19 pandemic, for example, altered and transformed people's lives in many ways very quickly. Businesses suffered major blows and people's habits and routines changed. Jobs were modified and the patterns and habits of individuals were altered as some technology-driven businesses discovered. Relationships and interactions dropped like dominoes with the national shutdown.

This national crisis brought change but also the prospect for long-term transformation altering the entire form and structure of how people work and relate. Basically, transformations can move systems from one stage to another, and alter their general character. Leadership must look beyond the present to what is unfolding in terms of future global research and scientific modifications.

What the future brings is an essential issue for business. Obviously, technology and the Internet are major influences. Without understanding what forces are at play politically and economically, business as usual can result in negative consequences. A major profitable company must adapt and adjust to change in order to remain successful.

In 2012, Denmark's largest energy company, "Danish Oil and Gas," confronted a financial crisis as the price of natural gas slid by 90 percent. The new CEO realized that this was an opportunity for fundamental change and the company was renamed to Ørsted.

The radical transformation meant rebuilding "a new core business and find new areas for sustainable growth." They moved from a "black" company interested in oil and gas to a "green" one concerned with wind energy. "In an era of relentless change, a company survives and thrives based not on its size or performance at any given time but on its ability to reposition itself to create a new future, and to leverage a purpose-driven mission to the end. That's why strategic transformation may be the business leadership imperative of the 21st century."[10] The trickle-down effect of energy concerns affects transportation, heating, manufacturing, construction, and other enterprises.

Major issues modify perspective and point of view, causing people to assess their priorities, spending, and investments, with a shift of perspective from the present to the future. Governments also address major challenges and pass legislation that may or may not be friendly to priorities and solutions. Politicians debate the present without knowing what will evolve in the future. The question politically is what priorities should politicians and others pursue—the past or the future?

To succeed long term, businesses and organizations require an understanding of the present factors affecting their operation, as well as a vision of what is unfolding in the immediate and long-term future with its possibilities and uncertainties. This is essential. Values in these businesses may remain the same or be altered based on planning for continued future success. Transformations also involve shifts in management operations and how business processes, people, and systems conduct their affairs.

Laszlo[11] identified four phases of major "macroshifts" or transformations, some of which are positive and others not. They include:

1. *The Trigger Phase*—technologies bring greater efficiency.
2. *The Transformation Phase*—technology changes social and environmental relations and increases production, faster growth of population, greater societal complexity. It also has a growing impact on the social relationships and the natural environment.
3. *The Critical [or Chaos] Phase*—pressure is placed on established culture, questioning established values and the ethics and ambitions connected to them. Society becomes chaotic and confronts two possible options:
   a. *The Breakdown Phase*—the values and ethics of a critical mass of people in society resist change or changes too slowly, and established institutions are too rigid to transform. Society is exposed to a series of crises that can degenerate into conflict and violence.

OR

   b. *The Breakthrough Phase*—The mindset of a critical mass of people shifts society to an adapted mode to improve social order and govern by more adapted values, worldviews, and associated ethics. As a consequence, the social system stabilizes itself and its changed conditions..

Economic transformation involves several basic areas: structural change and how, where, and when work gets accomplished. A major one is productivity that moves labor and other resources to generate cost-effective products and services more quickly and easily.

With technology, organizational structure and management practice are the foremost areas that affect productivity. Today, technology causes economic transformation. With it, change is not always linear but more cyclical and less predictable: very quickly altering communication, economic processes, access to knowledge, security, foreign affairs, and a wide swath of society.

Certainly there is flexibility in where and when people use technology for work or personal issues, as well as productivity and work culture. Like every other innovation, technology has implications. Stress increases as people feel the need to succeed or meet the expectations of others. Work can be all-consuming as technology creates the flexibility to work almost anywhere. People become addicted to their phones and are less attentive to external or personal relationships and requirements. Emotional and intellectual stress has reciprocal physical effects—headaches, neck and back issues, and even hearing and sight concerns, along with the deterioration of relationships.

Building informal relationships is difficult and "team" building is certainly more challenging as work has moved online, in texts, or on cell phones. The impact on individuals' work and personal lives also changes. Building deep personal relationships and friendships is more difficult working online or constantly using phones or other technology.

Today, connections and technology are quite easy. However, significant relationships require much more. One's life is more than an Internet connection because it is deeper and intimate, complete with all the human intellectual and emotional qualities. People need human connection and understanding. Energy and commitment come in being together physically, emotionally, and intellectually.

NOTES

1. Jamie L. Vernon, "Understanding the Butterfly Effect," *American Scientists* 105, no. 3 (May–June 2017).

2. Henry Mintzberg, *The Rise and Fall of Strategic Planning* (New York: The Free Press, 1994), 175.

3. Ron Ashkenas, "We Still Don't Know the Difference between Change and Transformation," *Harvard Business Review*, January 2005.

4. Marcel Chaudron, "Change vs. Transformation," https://rocknchange.com/change-vs-transformation/.

5. Irvine Laszlo, *Macroshift: Navigating the Transformation to a Sustainable World* (San Francisco: Berrett-Koehler Publishers, 2001), xv.

6. Peter Drucker, "The Age of Social Transformation," *The Atlantic*, December 1995, https://www.theatlantic.com/past/docs/issues/95dec/chilearn/drucker.htm.

7. Robert J. Samuelson, "How 'Long Economic Waves' Could Save Capitalism," *Washington Post*, June 14, 2020.

8. PEW Research, "Changes in the American Workplace," https://www.pewsocialtrends.org/2016/10/06/1-changes-in-the-american-workplace/.

9. Jonathan Haidt and Tobias Rose-Stockwell, "The Dark Psychology of Social Networks," *The Atlantic*, December 2019.

10. Scott Anthony, Alasdair Trotter, and Evan I. Schwartz, "The 20 Top Business Transformations of the Last Decade," *Harvard Business Review*, September 24, 2019.

11. Laszlo, *Macroshift*, 12–13.

Chapter 2

Personal Transformation

People feel isolated and cut off. Perhaps this is why the whole nation can assemble around the image of celebrities. They have no acquaintance with the celebrities personally. They look at them from a distance and project all the belongings onto them. When something happens to a celebrity they feel as if it is happening to themselves. There is an acute need for the reawakening of the sense of community.

—John O'Donohue

If people are apathetic, defeated in spirit, or unable to imagine a future worth striving for, the game is lost.

—John Gardner

Life itself involves transformations: birth to childhood to adulthood to aging. Over these times, human beings transform physically, intellectually, and socially. A young person who was just a face in the crowd transforms into a person who becomes a leader or innovator through commitment, character, and intelligence.

On this journey, individuals profoundly change their reason for living and the way they live. Experiences, thinking, and self-examination create a whole different life: past goals and missions are reshaped to reflect more closely their values and beliefs, as well as their dreams. A person's mindset and attitude are foremost in determining how they react to internal and external circumstances.

Lives do not move at the same pace through each stage. Experiences once deemed small and insignificant turn out to be life changing. The unexpected meeting with another person, a slight change in work responsibility, or other routine or unanticipated experience becomes highly significant.

Philosophical, emotional, spiritual, and intellectual transformations require each person to answer two fundamental questions: "Who am I?" and "Why am I here?" In doing so, individuals define who they are, what they stand for, and what provides direction and meaning in their lives. Self-understanding and self-reliance are necessary to develop and direct the future.

Basically, answering the "who" question determines what life is about in all its phases: sculpting each person through a multitude of circumstances physical, intellectual, psychological, and educational. Almost every person can highlight a situation, both positive and negative, that molded and informed their life and opened doors to the future.

The impact of those events comes clear: listen to children who had a parent die when they were young and the effect it had on their emotions and outlook, as well as their dependence and independence, as they worked their way through the decades. Finding oneself in and through these situations is difficult, and may take time because they are powerful and complicated. In the jigsaw puzzle of life, a piece is always missing.

DEFINING MOMENTS

Defining moments are turning points that change life's trajectory. These times are pivotal, and significantly redefine one's life and priorities. Defining moments can be swift or take time to come to realization. In many cases, they include the following steps:[1]

- A disorienting dilemma
- Self-examination, sometimes with feelings of guilt or shame
- Recognizing one's discontent and the process of transformation shared with others
- Exploration of new roles, relationships, and action
- Critically processing assumptions behind each decision
- Provisionally trying new roles
- Planning a course of action
- Acquiring knowledge and skills to pursue one's plan
- Building competence and self-confidence in new roles and relationships

Renewal is a part of everyone's life. Significant events formulate a person's perspective and personality. While many people experience similar circumstances, the response of and impact on the individual may differ substantially because of their uniqueness. No two lives are exactly the same: personality, creativity, and emotion are distinctive to each individual.

Transformation results in peak experiences, which basically are moments of clear insight and revelation about one's life. Individuals garner a new perspective, and with that come choices to select a new path or sustain the present one. In these times, dissonance and fears emanate from uncertainties, diverse interpretations, and past experiences. These conditions place the responsibility on individuals to address their life and what they desire it to be.

Beginnings and endings are a part of everyone's life: nothing lasts forever. An individual's role and responsibilities modify and evolve. One cannot be an athlete or physician forever. Ironically, endings give birth to new beginnings as alternative choices and perspectives arise. New people and situations appear and learning and knowledge awaken curiosity and passion. Insights can be transformational, and happiness is not one-dimensional.

All people confront emotional and economic hardships and obstacles: no one is immune to these times. While individuals are not always in control of what happens to them, power rests over how they respond. Difficulty opens eyes of understanding and windows of wisdom, if anger and fear do not paralyze thought and insight. Butterflies come alive in individuals' decisions, creating positive or negative consequences through emotion, reflection, and judgment, as well as timing.

CHAOS

Chaos happens. Minor events produce huge changes and eruptions. Weather, for example, is a chaotic system: so are the economy and politics. Control is not inherent and all these systems can be influenced by small and not always logical impulses.

Chaos can stagger mental models and processes. For individuals, chaos is a part of their lives because passion, unexpected interactions, and emotion can cloud logic and either resolve issues or instigate movement and instability of the norm.

In chaotic times, people understand that change is possible: some wanted and some resisted. With change, substituting one process for another is the norm. Basically, doing the same thing but with different processes or equipment, for example, using computers rather than typewriters to communicate on paper.

Chaos is created when things do not unfold in a straightforward manner—simple cause and clear effect. Life is unpredictable at times. Minor events have major implications, and sometimes random and unpredictable behavior occurs in complex systems.

Each person decides the path they take in chaotic times. Some perceive life events as a coherent sequence and others see them as nonlinear and sometimes a bit random. To some, serendipity happens! Chaos materializes and unforeseen and small events move individuals off course or in circles. The episodes, however, can open unique possibilities and unanticipated results.

Uncertainty is unsettling and transformational times raise apprehension about decisions and the future. Looking back many people never thought things would turn out the way they did. Not everything in life is certain: there is no predetermined blueprint, but choices are available. Some will work and others not. Planning becomes a victim of circumstances—some subtle and many beyond cognitive control.

Struggle provides a time for individual retrospection and introspection to determine who one is and what they represent and desire in life. Strength develops in these periods where, like butterflies, individuals transform and metaphorically mature as they gain understanding and insight. This process does not happen overnight—it takes, at times, short steps to gain perspective and sometimes only in retrospect do people understand.

The familiar is secure and comforting—knowing what exists and what is coming down the road. In deeply changing times apprehension arises on a number of fronts. Obviously, comfort and knowing what to do in these situations can dissipate as conditions become cloudy, complex, and tenuous. Not being sure of protocol instigates unrest and distrust.

Decisions can alter or determine the path to success or failure in a number of ways. After all, decisions raise questions: nothing is absolutely certain. Business and employment change, and the economy becomes the subject of different tangible and intangible forces. Society and relationships bring issues of safety, security, and opportunity. The anxiety of losing relationships or being rejected is intense because individuals want and need to be acknowledged. The relationship between being an independent individual and being accepted is not always easy.

In 2011, Denzel Washington[2] gave a graduation speech at the University of Pennsylvania. He stated,

> Well, here it is: I have found that nothing in life is worthwhile unless you take risks. Nothing.
>
> Nelson Mandela said: "there is no passion to be found playing small, and settling for a life that's less than the one you're capable of living."
>
> I'm sure in your experiences in school . . . in applying to college . . . in picking your major . . . in deciding what you want to do with life—people have told you to make sure you have something to "fall back on." Make sure you got something to fall back on. But I never understood that concept, adding something to fall back on.
>
> If I'm going to fall, I don't want to fall back on anything, except my faith. I want to fall forward. At least I figure that way I'll see what I'm about to hit. Fall forward.
>
> Here's what I mean: Reggie Jackson struck out 2600 times in his career—the most in the history of baseball. But you don't hear about the strikeouts. People remember the home runs. Fall forward.

Failure, however, is a part of change and, if they are wise, individuals learn from it. Without failure, introspection and growth do not take place. Blaming others or conditions does not lead to progress or success because attitudes become sour and creative action restricted. Falling into a victim mentality of blaming others is not being true to oneself because blaming others negates one's ability, talent, and perseverance. Success is built on failure if one is astute about life and its challenges.

People control their actions and responses. Self-examination and reflection on decisions are important. Playing the victim is not productive and does not solve issues: power comes from individual commitment to live one's principles through example and obligation. Success comes from working, not blaming others. After all, all individuals control their own perspective and decisions.

Failing is an opportunity to discard ideas or tactics that are no longer effective or useful: it opens eyes to a new reality and allows leaving the comfort of old patterns and practices to pursue different paths. It unties the knots of the status quo and releases individuals to explore and confront their perceptions and behavior sometimes involving their personal reinvention or generating new goals, thinking, and relationships.

PERSPECTIVES ON CHANGE

While change is evident in life, the reaction to it is not universal. The same is true for transformation as it becomes more clearly apparent. Not everyone stands up and gives the unfolding future a standing ovation, particularly when the total pattern and impact are uncertain.

World War II brought major transformations to the nation and life across all national borders. The pain of the war's transformational experience was long and deep and cost millions of lives and destroyed any sense of normalcy. With things beyond individual control, people dreamed of a brighter future. Citizens wanted to get back to "normal," although a new "normal" was unfolding slowly. The war brought to light transformative innovation in transportation, atomic energy, communications, national priorities, and stature, as well as international relations and the power of propaganda.

Even constructive transformations come with positive and negative repercussions.

Change or transformation does not bring uniform responses or agreement about the reordering and renovating that unfolds.

Some people are indifferent, which is not helpful when the world is changing before everyone's eyes. Those who are indifferent can become victims because of their lack of responsibility in examining the personal and social implications and consequences of policies and values. Indifference is not an antidote to transformation because it eliminates or forestalls any sense of responsibility to gain insight or act.

Three perspectives are evident in these circumstances. One is looking back and wanting to maintain the way things are or used to be: basically, the desire to revert to what was. People experienced the past and are familiar with it, while the future and what it brings is unknown and not clearly predictable. It quakes the spirit and energizes fear.

A second perspective is defending the status quo: focusing on doing more of the same. Just "keep at it!" and everything will be fine. In essence, the need for transformation is unnecessary because what we have can be improved and is generally working. After all, "We got this far by doing things this way. If we change, we might lose what we got through hard work."

A third perspective is advocating for a collective transformation, examining and understand patterns of the past, and beginning to promote the "highest future possibility."[3] Some are excited about the potential prospects, and the desire to pursue change, enhance the future, and think anew. However, transformation is not necessarily positive if it is predicated on biases, fears, and retribution.

People are skeptical of transformation because its impact is broad and not totally known or foreseeable. Relationships and individual character including values, ethics, morality, and motivation are affected. The consequences raise difficult and significant questions because standards or principles are affected. Ethical questions, the common good, and what is right and moral are involved. People are personally, socially, and politically influenced.

Philosophical issues, while abstract, have tangible consequences. Citizens must confront altered structures and conditions and even personal interactions, including how people think and react to things. Acting on established mindsets, approaches, dilemmas, and consequences may not be as effective in new and changing times. Conventional perspectives as well as processes and procedures are challenged.

MULTIPLE LIVES

People live two lives simultaneously: externally and internally. One is based on how others perceive them and what is expected of them to be accepted by the group or to meet the preferences of others. The perspective of peer groups and significant others is powerful. People want to be accepted, and at times, they engage in activities just to be liked and included, which may not meet their own desires, values, or ambition. Dissonance exists between what others want from them, and what the person believes in order to live with integrity to their individual values and needs. Independence is important to find a path to discovering and improving one's calling and mission in life.

The other life is inside their own mind: how they view themselves today and what they want to be in the future. Leading a life one desires calls for the courage to step out and follow an independent path. Fulfilling one's life and finding meaning is not a selfish act, but one of self-fulfillment and actively applying talents and skills. Sometimes, individuals need to be the "lone wolf howling in the wilderness" to fulfill their uniqueness and needs. And, in these circumstances, new perspectives and paths can open.

Personal transformation requires self-assessment and reviewing one's beliefs and assumptions, as well as internal needs, to find meaning. Their view of their life's path can change in order to determine a sense of what is personally and socially significant. For this to happen courage is required and the environment has to be conducive. Introspection cannot take place in the cacophony of threat or conflict.

Tough-minded optimism and belief in oneself is essential. Life is demanding and, sometimes, it is tumultuous. Confidence in one's beliefs and values are critically important. Time may require more than thought. Apathy produces dry rot and passive rejection of one's values and principles.

Success is never assured, but not living with integrity to one's beliefs and ambitions is the road to pretense and fabrication. Action and commitment can move situations in the right direction. Wholeness exists when beliefs, words, and actions are in harmony.

Integrity and credibility require self-reflection. It is much easier to engage in self-denial and deflection, rather than look inward. Introspection takes a conscious effort. People prefer to see themselves as they want to be seen by others. Self-reflection raises uncomfortable issues of self-acceptance and satisfaction with the choices and outcomes in one's life. Being true to oneself, even if it means standing alone, has consequences for self-acceptance and honor.

The courage to step forward, find contemplative space, and risk change is necessary for growth and learning. Everyone must confront doubts and anxieties, otherwise they can become barriers that imprison individuals from reaching out with integrity. Diversions and social distractions impede any self-examination.

Individuals living authentically to their beliefs and values have the power to be "one of a kind." Going along with the crowd or the impressions or needs of other individuals is rejected in order to find true significance and living with integrity in their own lives. With age they realize time is short and there are few opportunities to pursue what is significant and important to them. Living one's life to please others is empty and self-destructive.

A person's presence speaks louder and more personally. All people have had the need to have someone listen and simply be there for them. Everyone requires understanding and empathy, particularly during difficult conditions and experiences. Presence is powerful because it demonstrates caring and nonverbal connection and demeanor, as well as verbal and physical support.

Presence is more than being there physically. Peter Senge et al., stated:

> We've come to believe that the core capacity needed to access the field of the future is presence. We first thought of presence as being fully conscious and aware in the present moment. Then we began to appreciate presence as deep listening, of being open beyond one's preconceptions and historical ways of making sense. We came to see the importance of letting go of old identities and the need to control and, as Salk said, making choices to serve the evolution of life. Ultimately, we came to see all these aspects of presence as leading to a state of "letting come," of consciously participating in a larger field for change. When this happens, the field shifts, and the forces shaping a situation can move from re-creating the past to manifesting or realizing an emerging future.[4]

A fresh perspective of what is emerging from science, the creative arts, and the visual context emanates from change and transformation. Stopping habitual ways of thinking is necessary at times. Becoming aware of mental models and helping people think and perceive reality are necessary to realize what changes are taking place. It is necessary to get out of one's routine, engage with new individuals, examine areas of interest outside of work, and renew ideas and see connections, if any. Synthesis is an important skill.

CONTEXT

Context concerns relationships and personal transformations, as do economic and social forces because they present the stage upon which people must live and respond. The effect of each type of external transformation has an impact on people. Economics affects employment and cash flow. Resources become limited to pursue interests and thus the safety and security to confront the future. The economy and culture can destroy ambitions, current conditions, and future prospects.

Loneliness has risen as a concern, due in part to the rise of technology. The allure and constant presence of technology distracts people from being in the present moment and make individuals feel that they are "out of the mix" if they see their colleagues involved with others through technology or in person. To some, being connected, even if it's over the Internet, has become important, more so, in some cases, than physical presence. The focus on technology can also be rude and disrespectful.

Personal relationships are influenced by technology. First, it is much easier to stay in contact with people through phone calls, texts, or emails. However, making true connections requires much more than tapping on a keyboard and texting. Creating close social bonds is more difficult over technology than face-to-face relationships because the subtleties of spoken and nonverbal feelings and energy are not easily communicated online. The energy between people is lost over technology. "Being there" involves more than sound and a visual image. An individual's energy and physical presence does not easily get transmitted through voice or video or FaceTime.

John O'Donohue stated, "The more we become immersed in technology, the more difficult it is to be patient with the natural unevenness and unpredictability of living. We learn to close ourselves off, and we think of our souls and minds no longer as presence but more in terms of apparatus and function. Functionalist thinking impoverish presence. The functionalist mind is committed to maintenance and efficiency."[5]

Technology has also diminished the space people have between work and leisure. Pursuing leisure is difficult because technology is constantly available upon which they can work, be productive, or find distraction. While the Internet can easily bring "things" to people, it also creates polarization and leads to isolation and living in intellectual and informational silos.

Technology, ironically, creates personal and emotional distance that disrupts face-to-face conversations and relationships. But that issue also affects adults as vibrating phones, ubiquitous television, and anticipation of calls or texts easily distract them. External issues and motivation too often preclude human connections and individual needs and purpose. Boundaries of work and leisure break down in many cases. Parents express concern over children's attention spans and the prospect of their being addicted to their phones, iPads, computers, and other technology.

Technology has made "doing" pervasive, limiting simply "being"—presence involves awareness, feeling, heart, and soul, as well as the passion and emotion, in things outside the sphere of work and profession. Technology has created "The need to fill empty time for the sake of being productive, the constant rush in a race of accomplishment, and the compulsiveness of consumption of goods as means to an end."[6] In addition, the lure of entertainment, Facebook, Twitter, and other technology has the qualities of addiction.

Individuals get lost in work and technology and do not have time to discover or pursue their inner desires and interests. Happiness cannot be bought and fulfillment comes from family life and work, but also in exploring one's true self through experience and adventure—curiosity and ambition are invisible sources of contentment and gratification.

Social transformation creates a different context in terms of relationships, along with norms and values, acceptance or rejection, security or fear, and relationships or loneliness.

Ethics and values are the foundation for a civil society. Technology raises many issues about norms and principles. Because something can be done does not mean it should be done. Technology, for example, makes communication to the masses easier, but it can also prohibit free speech and be used for silencing minority opinions and perspectives. In today's society, these concerns expose the behavior of individuals, as well as major technology and Internet companies.

People individually or collectively are responsible for many transformations. Philosophers and others examine and purport ethics and values. Artists provide visual, auditory, and literary commentary. Scientists and inventors discover ideas and new dimensions for social, individual, and economic growth by following their interests and mission.

Transformation, like the metamorphosis of the butterfly, is thorough and its impact involves a wide swath of life from beginning to end. It changes things into something different or totally new usually through a developmental process or an event—it involves a broader sweep of change in all facets of life. History is a running record of transitions and transformations. They are inevitable. The question is: will they be positive and ethical in promoting knowledge and life?

NOTES

1. Devine Casondra and William L. Sparks, "Defining Moments: Toward a Comprehensive Theory of Personal Transformation," *International Journal of Humanities and Social Science* 5, no. 5 (March 2014).

2. Denzel Washington, University of Pennsylvania Commencement Ceremony, May 16, 2011.

3. Otto Scharmer, *Theory U: Leading from the Future as It Emerges* (San Francisco: Berrett-Koehler Publishers, 2009), 19.

4. Peter M. Senge et al., *Presence: An Exploration of Profound Change in People, Organizations, and Society* (The Crown Publishing Group, 2005), Kindle edition. Loc. 230.

5. John O'Donohue, *Eternal Echoes* (New York: Cliff Street Books, 1999), 75.

Chapter 3

Innovation

The Big and Small Picture

One can choose to go back safely or forward toward growth. Growth must be chosen again and again; fear must be overcome again and again.

—Abraham Maslow

We cannot solve our problems with the same thinking we used when we created them.

—Albert Einstein

To innovate, individuals require vision and the ability to question conventional wisdom. Passion and problem solving are needed to pursue ideas and discover the advantages and limitations of possibilities.

A curious intersection exists between science and the arts. Scientists investigate theories and concepts and search for the truth through research and trials. Data based decision making is the norm. Artists of all sorts envision possibilities, concepts, and perspectives through imaginative details, projections, and thought. Creative freedom brings forth vestiges of what is and what can be. New viewpoints and ideas come from both styles of examination and reflection.

Atlantic magazine published an article, "The 50 Greatest Breakthroughs since the Wheel," which discusses how twelve scientists, entrepreneurs, engineers, and historians of technology examined which innovations have done the most to shape the nature of modern life.[1] These individuals cited innovations independently, and then they were categorized into functional categories of the entire group.

The categories, along with the specific innovations, included:

- Innovations that expand the human intellect:

- The printing press, paper, Internet, personal computer, semi-conductor electronics, photography
- Innovations that are integral to the physical operating infrastructure:
  - Electricity, sanitation systems, air conditioning, cement
- Innovations extending life:
  - Nitrogen fixation (agriculture), penicillin, vaccination, sanitation systems, refrigeration, optical lenses
- Innovations that allow real-time communication:
  - The Internet, telegraph, telephone, radio, television
- Innovations in the physical movement of people and goods
  - Internal combustion engine, automobiles, airplanes, rocketry, compass, sextant
- Organizational breakthroughs:
  - The alphabet, Gregorian calendar

Obviously, innovations of the past were not always based on machinery or technology. Looking back, paper, pens, and the printing press involved the sharing of ideas and principles through letters, books, and newspapers. All of them had great impact on culture and knowledge. Today mechanization and technology are dominant innovations in the last hundred or more years of social, economic, and international history, including warfare.

Life and society are complex. No innovation is free of problematic and possibly disastrous consequences. The positive impacts of most innovations are obvious. However, there are downsides to every innovation, including artificial intelligence. Frequently cited is the loss in jobs, with no guarantee there will be enough good ones in the future for those presently working.

A widening gap between the rich and poor is also a possibility. As Joel Mokyr, who was involved in the *Atlantic* study, stated, "You look at antibiotics, insecticides, transportation—every time we saw one problem, a new one comes up. Each invention relies on subsequent inventions to clean up the mess made."[2] The issue concerns what positive innovation brings and an understanding that some changes may be difficult, but the correct thing to do.

NATIONAL IMPACT

Technology is a significant issue economically, politically, and personally. Innovation is a powerful force on the changes that are taking and will take place in all segments of society. Economic and productivity growth are critical national goals. To maintain America's standing in these areas depends on the ability to create, develop, and apply new ideas and technology. This must occur at the national, as well as the state levels, and eventually in each individual's personal life. Transformation affects them all.

Technological change produces leadership challenges. According to the National Academies of Sciences, Engineering, and Medicine, several trends exist in the competitive market.[3] Leaders and people generally do not have to be technological experts, but they must certainly understand the impact of innovation on democratic values and principles, as well as on individuals' independence and liberty. Technology for national security and competitiveness becomes increasingly dependent on innovation and its application.

Technological impact grows and accelerates in manufacturing and service industries as well as national security. Increased technological advancement among industrialized nations makes this essential. Internationalization of economic and technological application increases the interdependence of national economies.

Technological development, product, and service companies highlight the optimal use of human talents in the workplace: intelligence and creativity are at a premium. Complications, however, surface for the United States' continued growth in applying technology to maximum advantage. Major concerns include:

- Insufficient investment in workforce training and education for technological transformation.
- Inadequate investment by companies in competitive production processes, facilities, and equipment.
- Insufficient awareness of technology by companies originating outside their institutional boundaries.
- Lack of integrating technology policy with federal, domestic, and foreign economic policy so that there are effective working relationships between the private sector and government.

America's leadership internationally is based on federal investment in infrastructure and education, benefiting from a talent pipeline, and opening new markets and trade.

Today several things have changed affecting countries' technological leadership.[4] First, the pace of innovation has accelerated. A second issue is that the private sector technology companies that design and construct them do so in complex supply chains across the globe. In addition, China has mobilized economic ability rivaling that of the United States. Competition is certainly enhanced. In fact, American efforts "to accelerate innovation in critical frontier technologies, such as artificial intelligence and quantum information science, are so far too incremental and narrow in scale and scope."[5]

HOW AMERICANS SEE THINGS

Today, technology has an obvious impact on all citizens in the workplace, according to a study by the PEW Research Center.[6] How do citizens perceive the next thirty years?

- The public believes robots will take over much of the work done by humans, but most workers do not think it will affect their own type of work—82 percent believe much of the work presently done by humans will be completed by robots/computers.
- Seventy-six percent indicate that economic inequality between rich and poor will increase because of workplace automation.
- On balance, the public believes automation has done more harm than good for workers in the United States: 48 percent of all adults believe it has hurt American workers.
- Certain professions are viewed to be at greater risk of automation than others, e.g., fast food workers, insurance claims processors, software engineers, legal clerks, and others.
- Young adults are especially likely to be affected by workforce automation along with part-time workers.
- The public broadly supports workforce automation being limited to "dangerous and dirty" jobs.

Respondents obviously highlight issues that may affect them or their families and their future economic circumstances. In another PEW poll on "What Americans Expect the Future of Automation to Look Like,"[7] Americans anticipate a range of technological advances to occur in the next twenty years in the following areas:

- Seventy-nine percent believe doctors "probably will (58 percent)" or "definitely will (21 percent)" use computer programs to diagnose and treat most diseases.
- Sixty-five percent believe most stores will be fully automated and involve little human interaction.
- Sixty-five percent believe robots or drones instead of humans will make most deliveries in cities.
- Forty-two percent believe people in the future will create most of the products they buy at home using a 3D computer.

The Smaller Picture

Many conversations about transformation and technology focus on large issues of the economy, society, and politics. Major repercussions exist for individuals who cannot actually influence the changes that are taking place. They frequently perceive themselves as powerless—impotent victims at the mercy of corporate America and technology conglomerates.

Their sense of self-worth is threatened. Individuals need to make sense of their lives and find meaning. Respect is a major issue: both from others, as well as a sense of self-respect. For many, self-worth relates to family development and giving and providing care to others. Living a life based on positive principles and contributing to family and others is essential to feel that life has meaning.

Commitment to principles and values justifies life's purpose and actions. It does not mean wealth or fame, but simply living a "good" life based on standards of behavior and honorable ideals. For many individuals, this involves career, work, or calling where they contribute their talent and abilities and find satisfaction. Or, their work and contributions help and support positive results for others, in addition to their own families and greater community.

Unknown forces have considerable, unnerving impact. Today, the speculation about artificial intelligence and other technology reframing work and society generates uncertainty and anxiety. It seems that suddenly, life takes on science fictional accounts of the future; for example, machines that think far beyond completing a repetitive task to actually acting independently of human programming.

A sense of purpose is essential for all individuals to survive change and/or terrifying conditions. Viktor Frankl observed and shared in his book *Man's Search for Meaning* that purpose is fundamental to survival and to overcome harsh and terrifying events.

Frankl believes that meaning comes from creating work or doing positive deeds, from experiencing or encountering someone, or from the attitude people take when confronting unavoidable suffering. Frankl stated: "Everything can be taken from a man but one thing: the last of the human freedoms—to choose one's attitude in any given set of circumstances, to choose one's own way."[8] Choice is in every individual's hands: to try, to commit, to resist, to quit, and others. Choice is available throughout life when confronted by personal, social, political, or other ventures.

Personal transitions occur in life and change is evident. In these times, individuals may have to restructure their lives because of external social and economic events or movement, but also because some goals no longer provide meaning. In these cases, the impact on family life takes greater emphasis.

Supporting oneself and one's family is important in two ways. First, the loss of employment affects self-esteem and sense of purpose but also involves a loss of income and standing. Individuals feel a decline of control and a lost sense of efficacy. Happiness is different when control over one's life is lost. Meaning and happiness are connected.[9]

The erosion of meaning in transformational times is a major issue for people. Individuals can lose their sense of purpose, which affects their physical and mental health. Restructuring one's life may be necessary, including letting go of roles and skills that may no longer be necessary. "When their purposes are removed or cease to be viable sources of meaning, people suffer and soon find other purposes to shape and guide their lives and their daily activities."[10]

Living involves change: it is consistent with aging, family, career, and other aspects of life. Transformation, however, goes much deeper. The prospect of how to live, the forces at play, and viewpoint possibilities are altered. The old ground rules and prospects are no longer effective.

In the regular or experienced change, some semblance of comfort exists because the modifications were understood. When upcoming changes are known and expected, there is a clear history of the causes and patterns of them in professional, business, and the mechanics of life. Some even follow a linear progression: the seasons of the year, the pattern of aging, strategic business planning, and the logic of rational thought patterns.

Transformation—Impact

Transformation is much more deeply rooted and involves renovation in the "very condition of things" and is intended to "cause a metamorphosis in the form and structure."[11] Outward forms or inner character are altered. Transformation creates pressure on one's sense of purpose and efficacy as paradigm shifts occur. In these cases, people must adapt and change their thinking and perspective.

Transformation not only creates uncertainty and apprehension but also confusion because the thinking and mindset of the past may not be effective or useful in confronting the unexpected or unknown. The mindset about the forces at play, understanding the patterns, if any, and the required skills to comprehend and work in an evolving society, workplace, or world may not be apparent or available. In a chaotic system, linear plans may fail. This is true for organizations, as well as individuals. What is significant or insignificant is not always clear or known. Analytical and convergent thinking are necessary to generate different perspectives and ideas on what is unfolding and the consequences.

Transformational times create an uncertain future and world. Realizing that one's beliefs and assumptions may not be accurate or helpful is distressing. The fog of reform and transformation eventually lifts, but the process takes time and is not always painless.

Understanding that facing a future of transformation requires new ideas and knowledge is difficult and complicated. How does one gain the understanding and skills to be viable and successful in a world that no longer requires one's expertise or talent? Remember blacksmiths and the innovation of the machine?

In these times, Peter Senge et al. stated: "People don't just feel more out of control. They *are* more out of control. It's appropriate to feel some discomfort if they don't know where this (transformation) . . . will take them."[12] In these times, many people deny the transformational forces, as well as their personal feelings.

Individuals, however, must reevaluate their perspective of the future, which is not easy, especially if the present times are going well. Sensing and feeling what is happening, and observing sub-currents and influences must be defined, along with possible scenarios, in order to be able to understand and respond. A nonresponse and pretending "this too will pass" can be dangerous.

Transformational times raise questions in individual's minds about themselves—inside themselves.[13] How they perceive themselves personally that they frequently do not share with others. These questions include:

- Am I vulnerable? How safe am I? For many, they put on a façade or mask of confidence. However, these times push people to really ponder these questions and the ramifications.
- A second question and one related to the first is: Can I measure up and adequately confront the reality of the future? Issues of competence and a sincere concern for their career and future are interrelated.
- Finally, there is the factor of trust: self-trust in being able to adjust to new times, values, and expectations. Can I really change and succeed? Safety in one's analysis and actions is of concern because how and what works in new times is uncertain, as well as the unknown implications for self and family.

Facing an unclear future and learning how to approach it requires courage. No one really controls the future, but they can determine how they react to it. For many, this is a huge and uncertain step toward the future.

Some stability is necessary. The expectation that rules, principles, and policies remain stable is not always there. When organizations or individuals move in an entirely new direction, people often state, "This is a game changer" as past conditions or expectations are no longer valid, achievable, or reliable.

In reality, life is evolving relentlessly. Talking about the "old days" makes this apparent. Adapting and adjusting are a necessary aspect of life. The issue is that while life involves constant change, "meaning, on the other hand, is based on stability and permanence." There's a sense of "false permanence."[14]

Processes and conditions change, but the stabilizing force in life is commitment to ethics and positive principles. Transitions should not erase the concepts of "life, liberty and the pursuit of happiness." Those concepts are basic in discerning how transformation unfolds and exists. Identity is necessary for a stable life, while living true to one's values and principles.

In all of this, individuals need to know who they are—their authentic sense of self. People are more than bodies. While individuals' bodies are similar in structure and operation, their personal identities are far from the same.

Identity answers one question, "Who am I?," that refers to their interpersonal self, their roles and reputation, but also their ethics, priorities, and potential. While bodies change, identity involves being in harmony with values and principles.

Individuals do not live their lives for a claim or to meet the demands of others. They must understand they are unique and never to be duplicated. That is the responsibility all people have. It provides the basis for self-fulfillment.

NOTES

1. James Fellows, "The 50 Greatest Breakthroughs since the Wheel," *The Atlantic*, November 2013.

2. Ibid.

3. National Academic Press, "Mastering a New Role: Shaping Technology Policy for National Economic Performance," 1993, 1–2.

4. William McGraven, James Manyika, and Adam Segal, "America Faces Fresh Challenges to Technology Innovation Leadership," *The Hill*, September 18, 2019.

5. Ibid.

6. PEW Research, "How Americans See Automation and the Workplace," https://www.pewresearch.org/fact-tank/2019/04/08/how-americans-see-aut omation-and-the-workplace-in-7-charts/.

7. PEW Research, "What Americans Expect the Future of Automation to Look Like," https://www.pewresearch.org/fact-tank/2017/11/16/what-americans-expect-the-future-of-automation-to-look-like/.

8. Viktor Frankl, *Man's Search for Meaning* (Boston: Beacon Press, 1992), 65.

9. Roy F. Baumeister, *Meaning of Life* (New York: The Guilford Press, 1991), 218.

10. Ibid., 49.

11. James MacGregor Burns, *Transforming Leadership* (New York: Atlantic Buckley Press, 2003), 24.

12. Peter Senge et al., *The Dance of Change* (New York: Currency Doubleday, 1999), 242.

13. Ibid., 244.

14. Ibid., 99.

Chapter 4

Technology

Have I done the world good, or have I added a menace?

—Guglielmo Marconi

When digital transformation is done right, it's like a caterpillar turning into a butterfly, but when done wrong, all you have is a really fast caterpillar.

—George Westerman, MIT Sloan Initiative

When individuals look back, particularly those close to retirement, they reflect about how different life is than in the past. They also understand that time passes quickly, particularly, it seems, when things are going well. Time, however, moves at different tempos. When facing pain or personal disruption and uncertainty, the clock slows to an agonizing pace. In moments of emotion and deep and loving thought, time moves briskly.

Technological innovation pushes time with lightning speed in transportation, information, employment, and other social and commercial levels far beyond anything in prior times.

Speed has become a virtue. While that is true, innovation and its corollaries require time before major economic and social transformation result and become evident. Its adoption is more complicated and requires time and creativity. Understanding and discernment is required to determine the specific influence of an innovation or renovation. In addition, sometimes people do not have a clear perspective—or clue—about the ability or promise of new innovations. Not everyone clearly perceives the need or potential for change and reformation. Comfort, generally, resides in the familiar.

Several examples demonstrate how individuals, businesses, and industries in the past perceived inventions. A major one is Western Union, which had the opportunity to purchase Alexander Graham Bell's telephone patent for $100,000. Western Union refused the deal because it did not perceive the telephone as part of their business specter. They withdrew from the offer and, in exchange, Bell agreed to stay out of the telegraph business.

The potential of innovations is not always clear even from the standpoint of the inventor.[1] There is uncertainty. Gugliano Marconi invented the radio and thought it could be used "primarily to communicate between two points where communication by wire was impossible"—ship-to-ship communication. Marconi thought the market for the radio was with the steamship companies, other naval use, and newspapers. Broadcasting was not in Marconi's vision: narrowcasting was. Creative perspective is needed to discern the future potential and needs of transformative innovation.

Computer technology today is ubiquitous in all facets of life from work to daily needs to surgery to entertainment and more. While people take its availability for granted, it was not always perceived as universally practical.

In the 1940s after World War II, the first electronic digital computer had approximately 1,800 vacuum tubes and required a full room of space to house it. Having a small laptop in a coffee shop was not a reasonable possibility at that time. Computers were considered only for scientific research and rapid calculation, as well as data processing.

Thomas Watson, Sr., who was then president of IBM, rejected the idea that there was a large market for the computer."[2]

Many new technologies at the time of invention are primitive and the mindset in those circumstances may not perceive broader possibilities or the need to develop and apply them. Determining usefulness sometimes requires time and more invention.

With the computer, the creation of other innovations and discoveries was necessary to apply them more broadly. The computer in the late 1940s was not recognized to be a sound investment because its wider application was not thought possible until the transistor arrived. The transistor is a prime innovation that expanded the potential and the use of the computer across a wide swath of social, scientific, and economic life.

The commercial application of technologies instigates other innovations and, certainly, private sector investment. Rosenberg states, "New technologies, rather, need to be conceived of as building blocks. Their eventual impact will depend on what is subsequently designed and constructed with them. New technologies are unrealized potentials that may take a very large number of eventual shapes. What shapes they actually take will depend on the ability to visualize how they might be employed in different contexts."[3]

Transformations are generally not lightning strikes that change the world overnight. Of course, there have been historic events with consequences that altered life politically and economically; for example, the 2001 attack on the World Trade Center in New York, the stock market crash of 1929 (the Great

Depression), and certainly, the COVID-19 pandemic. The issue in these situations is clear and the response quick.

However, with innovation the change may be less direct and robust. Social, scientific, and cultural transformations have long-lasting effects—though they may be slower in formulating than unexpected historical events. The impact of innovation-driven transformation over time requires support, investment, and social understanding; for example, the loss of agricultural workers and the rise of industrial workers from 1900 to 1990, and the rise of knowledge workers replacing industrial employees and accounting for approximately a third of all workers. As the United States moved through these phases, there was a greater need for education because new employment skills were necessary. The link between transformation and education will certainly continue into the future.

According to Peter Drucker, knowledge workers will be the largest segment of the employee group.[4] A formal education is a doorway to these jobs. Some of them require highly developed manual and intellectual skills. Education is a major requirement for future jobs, much more so than in the past and as AI is applied in these industries. The possibilities with technology are seen in some eyes as a great opportunity to expand education and employees' abilities. The question is the nature of the growth and its requirements.

Peter Schwartz stated that the term "infinite possibility" describes the viewpoint that "growth was inevitable: abundance and unparalleled growth."[5] This attitude assumed that improvement and expansion would occur consistently over time. This seductive optimism fueled the computer industry and others over the decades.

While there are optimistic examples, the bright tomorrow may not be consistent or universal. Today, economically some are making a tremendous living, while others are losing their jobs. Drucker's analysis of the upcoming changes and reforms in employment highlight the possible "tomorrow" only for some or none at all.

Economists distinguish between two forms of innovation. One is process innovation, which results in less employment because of equipment or other approaches in how work gets done. Applying mechanics or technology to get the same work completed is a constant innovation throughout history.

The other form of innovation is product innovation, resulting in new products that lead to an increase in employment through a new way of solving problems, resulting in purchasing new equipment or material. Hence, increasing employment through innovation.

Joseph Schumpeter,[6] an economist, believed that innovation was a major factor in economic growth. Revolutionary change was at the core of economic development and moves the economy out of its static mode into a new era. New products, new methods, new sources of material, and new industrial structures create new approaches through entrepreneurship.

An employment gap can occur as a result of the changes and requirements for work, technology, and artificial intelligence. National and state governments will be pressured as technical and social transformations take place. As Americans and other nations confront significant transformation there will be winners and losers.

To respond to innovation, organizations and businesses engage in a process of "creative destruction,"[7] which simply means that innovation or change requires new approaches and directions because the old assumptions may not be valid anymore. Some jobs or procedures are eliminated so that new jobs and systems to meet evolving times can be added. In many cases, with technology, lower skilled jobs are replaced with fewer skilled and technology workers. However, some high skilled jobs may be replaced by artificial intelligence.

Change in perspective is necessary requiring rethinking and adapting to contemporary forces and knowledge. This can be done by systematic transition—maintaining current operations while developing and implementing new and creative approaches. Greater sophistication of these technologies will continue to challenge jobs.

Reducing employment in one area can result in increased employment in another. But not all consequences are positive. "A society cannot reap the rewards of creative destruction without accepting that some individuals might be worse off, not just in the short term, but perhaps forever."[8] This approach, while difficult for some individuals, allows the company and society to become more productive, competitive, and affluent overall. Transformative times are not unidirectional—to make gains sometimes requires taking losses for both companies and employees.

IMPACT ON PEOPLE

Earl was talking to his son, Curtis, about contemporary parenting. "Well, when I was a kid," Earl said, "parents didn't negotiate with kids about supper. You negotiate with them too much."

Curtis interrupted and said, "Yeah, dad, times are different now. Being raised right after World War II was a lot different than being raised today. My kids are not going to eat ham hocks and sauerkraut."

"That's for sure! Hey, when did they discover 'chicken nuggets' anyway? At least in the old days, you knew where the hocks came from." They laugh. "That was it! You ate what was put in front of you. Kids didn't negotiate for supper."

"Yeah, I know full well," his son replied.

"I can't believe what is happening to our society today! Kids need structure—they really do not understand life isn't always easy." He paused and looked at Curtis. "At times, I hear your Mom—my wife of thirty-five years—say to me, 'you know, you sound like an old person! Get over it!'" He laughed.

Curtis said, "You know, Dad, Mom may have a point!"

Times involving social and personal evolutions bring uncertainties, creating discomfort and, in some cases, distress. Sometimes age, generation, education, finances, or other factors influence the interpretation of circumstances and movements. Maturity brings a deeper understanding, if not a broader perspective, of social and economic change.

In times of transformation, some people become unsettled as they perceive things falling apart and established values and principles weakening. Looking back is easy and relatively clear. Looking ahead is unpredictable and ambiguous because personal and social forces are not always apparent or assessed properly.

Old pillars (values, ethics, standards) seem to be degenerating and the strengths and downsides of innovation are uncertain; creating anxiety, vulnerability, and even grief. Clarity and understanding—"knowing the ropes!"—provide a clear basis for decisions and successes in the past. In today's times, the "ropes" may not even be clearly evident or considered, creating confusion. What is the truth and the correct pathway?

Skepticism grows in times of reformation. Logic and reason of the past does not seem clear-cut for the present. The circumstances create a clash between reason and emotion. Reason wants to analyze and interpret, while heart-felt feelings and emotions produce a different interpretation of circumstances. Does logic from the past apply to times of transformation? Reason or feeling—which one takes precedence? Is AI reasoning always the right path to follow?

Transformations unfold with time. Periods of transition are distressing because the challenges are not always obvious and the direction cloudy: figuring out what is really happening and how to respond personally and socially is unclear. Stand pat? Go with the flow? Examine short-term possibilities? Wait?

These times often call for self-assessment and examination of the concerns and desires individuals have for self and family. Things feel out of control and beyond one's scope. Looking at the external world and determining one's reaction and role require thought, logic, and principles.

Each person must eventually respond. Playing the role of victim is inappropriate and destructive. Any semblance of maturity requires individuals to have some understanding that uncertainty is an aspect of life, and how to respond to these times.

Throughout every life-stage, experiences bring opportunities for learning and growth, as well as endings and uncertainty. Doubt and apprehension evolve in either case. Nothing is written in stone. Relationships develop and end: death is a part of life, just as birth is. New contacts and relations occur with evolution: jobs, personal relationships, neighbors, friends, commitments, education, institutions, and more. Relationships are essential because they are necessary for a sense of wholeness and connection.

As people progress through life they sometimes reminisce about "the good old days and the old way of doing things." Work and how it is completed has changed, particularly with technology. In many cases these modifications altered careers and opportunities. Times like these require adjustments, everyone must know "who they are" and how they find satisfaction and self-identity. People are not simply their jobs. Life is not static. New waves of knowledge and research deliver inventive understandings and concepts. Along with them come innovation and change.

PROCESS AND FEELINGS

Optimism is inherent in American culture as stated in the song from the musical *Annie*, "the sun will come out tomorrow." Optimism—deal with the cobwebs and sorrow, because tomorrow will be a better day. This has been an American mantra throughout the decades.

Today, polls illustrate that Americans are not very optimistic about the future on a number of fronts. While optimism is perceived to be an American trait, transformational times raise great doubt and pessimism that the future will supersede today's comfort and conditions and live up to its values.

PEW research polled Americans in 2019 about their perception of the future in 2050. "A narrow majority of US adults (56%) say they are somewhat or very optimistic about what the country will be like in 2050."[9] In specific areas, optimism is not evident, the results indicate:

- Most Americans expect income gaps to widen and a decline in living standards.
- The public sees tougher financial times on the horizon for older adults.
- The majority of adults are pessimistic about climate change and environment.
- Most Americans expect widespread job automation in the future—few see this as a good thing for the United States.
- Americans see a smaller role for the United States on the world stage.

- Americans expect political divisions to intensify, and many are worried about dysfunction in Washington.
- Partisans have starkly different ideas about what steps the federal government should take to improve life in the future.

TECHNOLOGICAL ANXIETY—WHY?

Ironically, the concerns about technology are actually based on the optimistic view of its growth and prospects in the future. The dark side of this optimism is the fear that technological growth will replace human labor with machines and technology, while increasing quality and service. Long-term impacts may be beneficial, but at a short-term cost in employment and loss of fiscal stability for some.

Accomplishments are not all good or moral. Human history demonstrates that very vividly. Innovation can be used for either, depending on the people in charge of its application. The concern is the growth of technology on the welfare of people can have dehumanizing effects. To some, a life of leisure is good and a life filled with work is negative. However, people find creativity and satisfaction in their work—if not there, then in some other endeavor. Fulfillment comes from the opportunity to make viable contributions to a project or larger community. Meaning is a powerful drive to happiness and personal realization.

A good life involves more than leisure: purpose, principles, and relationships matter. People want to be significant because being irrelevant and unneeded comes with serious emotional travails, and the loss of purpose and meaning. Each life is significant, as all humans are, because they have equal moral status and they pursue meaning through their love, interests, and benevolence. Meaningfulness actually involves goodness and being responsible.

LESSONS FROM THE PAST

Technological revolutions require social, scientific, and economic knowledge. History illustrates its impact. Innovation's impact can bring about transformation in many or all aspects of life. All of this requires investments and/ or social and political needs and consequences. Government involvement, depending on its nature, fosters or hinders these transformations.

Any society or system must examine the environment and context and adapt to the alterations and forces at play. Otherwise, like a caterpillar that doesn't transform into a butterfly, it dies.

Transformation brings about major transitions and revolutions. Values and principles reflected in the transformations can challenge issues of principle in their application relating to government policies, individual rights, and other circumstances. Values undergird individual, social, and corporate behavior and can raise conflict between and among them. New approaches and behaviors will be applied that can affect established relationships and norms.

Values and principles are constant stabilizing forces, which define the moral and ethical implications for the use and application of new technology and innovation. Values and principles should be a constant stabilizing force in society and governance. They formulate moral and behavioral standards for the use and application of policy and technology and in an upcoming age of artificial intelligence and learning machines.

With transformation, dialogue is necessary to listen to and understand the perceptions, needs, and fears of people. Things happen to individuals, but dialogue with people can help give them a voice, as well as greater understanding of the transformation that is evolving. Being heard and understood brings some solace and reassurance.

As Gandhi stated, "Be the change you wish to see in the world." The nature of change and transformation is dependent on individuals' understanding of values and principles to ensure that it moves in the right direction through proper course.

NOTES

1. Nathan Rosenberg, "Uncertainty in Technological Change," in *The Mosaic of Economic Growth* (Stanford University Press, 1996), 94.

2. Ibid., 94.

3. Ibid., 105.

4. Peter J. Drucker, "The Age of Social Transformation," *Atlantic Magazine*, December 1995.

5. Peter Schwartz, *The Art of the Long View* (New York: Doubleday, 1996), 154–55.

6. Karol Sledzik, "Schumpeter's You and Innovation and Entrepreneurship," *SSRN Electronic Journal*, April 2013.

7. Silva Glessia and Luis Carlo DiSerio, "The Sixth Wave of Innovation," *FEAUSP* 13, no. 2 (April–June 2016).

8. John Mauldin, "The Age of Transformation," June 2014, https://www.mauldineconomics.com/frontlinethoughts/the-age-of-transformation.

9. PEW Research, "Looking Ahead to 2050, Americans Are Pessimistic about Many Aspects of Life in US," https://www.pewresearch.org/fact-tank/2019/03/21/looking-ahead-to-2050-americans-are-pessimistic-about-many-aspects-of-life-in-u-s/.

Chapter 5

Artificial Intelligence

The real goal of AI is to understand and build devices that can perceive, reason, act, and learn at least as well as we can.

—Astro Teller, British Scientist

Today's grandchildren find it difficult to comprehend the life of their grandparents before the ubiquitous computers, cell phones, and televisions. They laugh when they hear stories of grandpa lying on the floor as a kid listening to the Cubs game on the radio, which was the size of a chest of drawers. It seems inconceivable to them to be without access to today's technology. In reality, however, that same perception will exist in the minds of their grandchildren in 2070.

Will transformation continue at the present rate or intensity and in what areas of life? What changes, outside of efficiencies or speed, can happen? Will a new age of thinking machines alter life beyond human imagination and control? Everything seems to be at people's fingertips today. The power of current technology certainly will increase, as well as its memory and access.

Andrew Yang, American entrepreneur and former presidential candidate, stated, "the world has changed; the world is changing. We can't put the genie back in the bottle, try as we might or wish as we might."[1] The issue may not be simply innovation, automation, efficiencies, and systems—but a much deeper issue of "smart" machines, analytics, and complex thinking. In the past those abilities were simply the domain of human beings. Science fiction and its human-like robots were simply viewed as unachievable fiction.

In the past, the limitations of the human body were overcome. Today, the challenge is more dramatic and intense. "We are overcoming the limitation of our minds. We're not getting rid of them, we're not making them unnecessary, but holy cow, can we leverage them and amplify them now. You have to be a huge pessimist not to find that profoundly good news."[2]

Artificial intelligence: the term itself seems suspect. Can intelligence really be artificial? Can it be created and manufactured? Historically, intelligence was perceived strictly as a human quality: complex and interwoven with perception, analysis, intellect, interpretation, evaluation, creativity, feelings, beliefs, and other means of comprehension and communicating. Intelligence is not a body part but a complex of mental reasoning and intellectual capacity, along with emotion, intuition, and wisdom. Can machines really garner all those abilities?

Artificial intelligence raises the question of nonhuman devices having the intelligence to consider issues, think, analyze, evaluate, and come to conclusions. If they do, can they make decisions? Does it have "smartness" and can it have a measured IQ, including rising to the level of genius? Even so, do geniuses always make the correct and moral decisions? Is cognitive intelligence sufficient?

According to the Cambridge dictionary "smart" is defined as intelligent or able to think quickly or intelligently in difficult situations. Merriam Webster condenses the definition to having or showing a high degree of mental ability. Both dictionaries allude to the concept of being witty and glib, in addition to being capable of rational thought.

In his book *Frames of Mind*, John Gardner detailed the theory of multiple intelligences that move beyond and much deeper than simple recall and memory. In earlier times, the response to these two abilities determined one's intelligence.

Gardner's theory of multiple intelligences specifies that intelligence is more diverse and complex than "smartness." He does so because reason, logic, intelligence, and knowledge "are not synonymous." The different aspects of intelligence as defined by Gardner "are relatively autonomous."[3] The intelligences he cites include: linguistic, musical, logical-mathematical, spatial, bodily-kinesthetic, and personal.

As individuals examine their own and others' lives, it becomes clear that skills, talent, and perspective, along with wisdom and understanding are not equally present. Differences in intelligence are obvious, as well as philosophies and beliefs that contribute to the development or suppression of one's talent and skills.

In a later book, *Five Minds for the Future*, Gardner highlights the fact that changes in society and the world require five minds to address challenges and circumstances. The following "minds" people must consider for success in the future include:[4]

- *The disciplined mind:* mastering a way of thinking in a specific scholarly discipline and formal education, e.g., mathematics, science, history, and other academics, as well as professional training.
- *The synthesizing mind:* selecting critical information from disparate sources, evaluating it, and making sense of it to self and others.

Recognizing new information and skills, and continuing the development of knowledge.

- *The creating mind:* puts forward imaginative ideas, configuring new questions, making judgments, and generating unexpected answers. Basically, thinking outside the box and offering creative insight and innovation.
- *The respectful mind:* responding sympathetically and constructively to others, working effectively with peers, understanding others' points of view, and creating a supportive environment.
- *The ethical mind:* acting consistently within one's role to fulfill one's responsibility in harmony with professional values, and thinking conceptually with the strength of character to build supportive relationships.

The pertinent issue is: can artificial intelligence think like a human being? People do not all think alike, they have both multiple and emotional intelligence. People need to reason, learn, problem solve, develop perceptions, and express themselves in language and other abstract, artistic, and theoretical means.

No one could survive in any culture without these abilities. Even if they lived an isolated life, people still require thinking and reasoning ability to problem solve, as well as understand the complications of their own perceptions and interpretation of situations.

HUMAN INTELLIGENCE

Human intelligence is not easy to define. Previously, for example, psychologists defined it as the ability to think abstractly—others emphasized learning and answering questions correctly. More recently, psychologists agreed that adaptations to the environment are important—learning to adjust to conditions and situations. Adapting is the ability to deal or cope more effectively with various interactions and issues throughout life.

Human intelligence includes learning from experience and making adjustments and modifications through perception, memory, learning, reasoning, and problem-solving. Intelligence does not simply involve a single ability. Intelligence, like other abilities, does not operate at the hyper preferred level all day, each day, or consistently over time. There are fluctuations based on time, conditions, and circumstances.

Human intelligence is strongly influenced by environmental factors. Genetics is an issue, but environment is also a significant factor. A child's home environment and parenting are consequential. Children require good nutrition and the availability of learning resources at their disposal. Another aspect of intelligence is being able to apply it in different and challenging circumstances. In other words, a sense of self-efficacy is necessary to confront issues and use their own intelligence to solve them. Addressing concerns, managing emotions, and applying thought and problem solving are necessary.

Reason is based on cognitive thought and logic. Other circumstances, however, affect intelligence and response. Sometimes individuals have an innate feeling or emotion that drives them to positive outcomes, even though statistics and logic may suggest otherwise.

Consciousness and insight move, at times, beyond black and white analysis. A sense of what is true comes down to perception, feelings, and beliefs. Some people think, however, that something is true if others or the media repeat it frequently. Truth and beliefs, however, are not necessarily synonymous. An educated person moves beyond beliefs and preferences.

Determining the truth entails moving beyond one's own perception and philosophy. Finding the truth demands thinking objectivity, understanding issues, and recognizing that relatively small issues can circumvent events and theories.

ARTIFICIAL INTELLIGENCE

Artificial intelligence is often perceived as something in the future, when actually it is quite evident today. Anyone using a cell phone is applying some form of artificial intelligence. Siri, for example, is a "virtual" assistant that can answer questions, make recommendations, and apply the Internet to get answers, using the phone, checking information and schedules, and searching the Internet. Siri was developed by the SRI International Artificial Intelligence Center and is a spinoff of the Department of Defense advanced research projects.

AI has moved from relatively simple tasks (Siri) to more complex thinking. Cognitive engagement moves the technology into areas only science-fiction writers considered. Marvin Minsky, an early pioneer of AI research back in 1970, stated, "In three to five years we will have a machine with the general intelligence of an average human being."[5] While scientists talk about the expansion of AI and its capabilities, not all citizens are clear or positive about its impact on their lives. In fact, some individuals find technology a complicated, unnecessary, and complex issue.

Today, artificial intelligence is everywhere. People take it for granted and often do not realize that it is being applied in so many other activities. How did it start?

In 1956, artificial intelligence was born at the Dartmouth Artificial Intelligence Summer Research Project. A generation of scientists was motivated to explore the potential of information technology to match the capabilities of humans.

One goal of this meeting was: "Automatic Computers—If a machine can do a job, then an automatic calculator can be programmed to simulate the machine. The speeds and memory capacities of present computers may be insufficient to simulate many of the higher functions of the human brain, but the major obstacle *is* not lack of machine capacity, but our inability to write programs taking full advantage what we have."[6]

Artificial intelligence covers a range of applications: from board games to algorithmic machines capable of thinking. John McCarthy coined the term in 1956 at an academic conference. Earlier in 1950 Alan Turing wrote a paper in the magazine *Mind*, "Computing Machinery and Intelligence," in which he discussed the implications of machines that could think.

While computers process logic, some individuals argue that it is not necessarily thinking. Understanding is more complex. Turing proposed an approach to determine whether or not machines could think, entitled the "Imitation Game." The test is based on the assumption "that a computer that is indistinguishable from an intelligent human" will actually demonstrate that machines can think.[7]

Another assessment, the Feigenbaum Test, evaluates whether a computer can pass as an expert in a particular field of study. In essence, the machine must solve problems that a live expert would be able to resolve. The idea was that if individuals cannot tell the difference between a human and a machine solving the situation, then it may prove that a computer can think. In addition to determining its ability, competition between humans and computers was conceived.

Competing with human experts has been completed in chess and the game called "Go," a popular chess-like game, which is played in China, Japan, and South Korea. Google's AlphaGo was a computer game that started with the rules of "Go," plus a database of historical games. AlphaGo was designed to teach itself, which was a form of artificial intelligence called "deep learning" that mimics the "neural networks of the human brain."[8]

AlphaGo was programmed with past games, learned moves, results, losses, victories, and strategies. From these, the computer figures its own moves and does not just follow programmed instructions. The computer analyzes results in tactics and approaches and then the AI system comes up with moves in strategy that humans have not created.

In 1997, Deep Blue, a chess computer built by IBM, beat Garry Kasparov, the world champion, in a six-game match. Deep Blue's processor had the capability to review two hundred million possible moves per second and project as many as six to eight or more plays ahead. Deep Blue, with its deep learning, made national news.

Deep learning concerns artificial intelligence's ability to imitate the workings of the human brain in processing data and information, and identifying patterns for possible future decision making. It recognizes speech, translates languages, and make decisions using big data from social media, economics, and a variety of Internet online sources. The extent of the data is enormous and would require decades for humans to process and analyze. Artificial intelligence requires the ability to acquire knowledge by identifying patterns in raw data, which can be a source of potential bias in machine learning. Raw data must be clear of any bias, and when and how the data was collected could be a problem.

Algorithms are critically important in this process. They program the computer to follow and analyze data sets and identify recurring patterns in the data. This provides the basis to make data-based decisions. "Deep learning enables data-driven decisions by identifying and extracting patterns from large data sets that accurately map from sets of complex inputs to good decision outcomes."[9]

Artificial intelligence involves simply more than computer science: it also involves philosophy, psychology, and other areas. Several characteristics make artificial intelligence more complex than simple computers.

One aspect of AI is big data: the capability of processing massive amounts of data, whether it is structured or unstructured. This is critically significant. Human beings would require a long time to process data of that magnitude.

The second aspect is the ability to learn based on historical patterns in data and input of experts into the feedback loop. Moving beyond learning, AI has the ability to reason, deductively or inductively, and draw inferences based on the data and circumstances. Context driven awareness is part of the system.

A major aspect of AI and one of some concern is problem solving through analysis for general or special purposes. Artificial technology has the ability to sense, reason, engage, and learn that will involve voice recognition, natural language processing, computer vision, robotics and motion, planning and optimization, and capture knowledge.[10]

Three levels of artificial intelligence are available:

- **ANI**—Artificial Narrow Intelligence: refers to a computer being able to do a single task very well, e.g., playing chess. Unlike general intelligence, narrow intelligence focuses on a single subset of abilities and looks to make strides in that area. ANI is fairly prevalent: automobiles are full of these systems, Google search is one large ANI brain, email spam filters are equipped with them, passenger planes are flown almost entirely by ANI.
- **AGI**—Artificial General Intelligence: reaches and passes the intelligence level of a human and has the ability to reason, plan, solve

problems, think abstractly, comprehend complex ideas, and learn quickly from experience. AGI concerns the emerging field of "Thinking Machines"—general-purpose systems with intelligence comparable to that of humans. The advantage of AGI is speed, storage in which computers memorize more things with reliability and durability in seconds than a human can in ten years. It has collective capability because it is not biologically constrained to one body, will not have cooperation problems, and can synchronize and update its operating systems.

- **ASI**—Artificial Super Intelligence: an intellect that is much smarter than the best human brain in practically every field including scientific creativity, general wisdom, and social skills. In the future this level of artificial intelligence is likely to remove the distinction between human intelligence and machines. ASI machines will be able to perform extraordinary things that only humans are capable of. They will be competent in decision making, art, and even emotional relationships. . . . Any human attempt to constrain it will be unreasonable."[11]

Artificial intelligence in its various levels will create transformations across various aspects of contemporary life. They are evident in transportation, leading to autonomous vehicles on the roads. In addition manufacturing involves robots working with humans to complete work in assembling and warehousing. Healthcare involves artificial intelligence concerning diagnosis, drug discovery, virtual nursing, and the application of the data personalizing medical practice.

In education, tutorial services are available, along with customizing teaching methods and content for students. The media employs Cyborg technology for understanding complex financial reports and for the production of reports and stories.

Obviously, with customer service artificial intelligence is incorporated in enhancing telephone calls, booking appointments, and similar service systems.

Artificial intelligence processes large amounts of data far more quickly than humans can. Huge amounts of data collected every day is far beyond what can be managed by a team of researchers. AI, using machine learning, is able to do that and develop information on which actions are possible. But this ability comes with a cost—it can be highly financially expensive.

Weak AI is assigned to complete a specific task: individual robots for example or virtual assistance like Siri. Strong AI, also known as artificial general intelligence (AGI), on the other hand, replicates the cognitive abilities of the human brain. When confronted with an unfamiliar task, it applies knowledge by itself from another domain to find solutions.

Humans and strong AI use three cognitive skills. First, the learning process is essential to analyze and complete specific tasks. That is where algorithms come in. Acquiring data and information and creating rules for turning hard data into actionable information is done through algorithms, which define the approach—step-by-step guidelines to analyze and complete specific tasks.

Artificial intelligence also learns by trial and error, examining different approaches until the solution is found. "Simple memorizing of individual items and procedures—known as rote learning—is relatively easy to implement on a computer. A more difficult problem is 'generalization,' which involves applying past experiences to analogous new situations."[12]

A second cognitive skill is reasoning, which concerns drawing appropriate deductive or inductive inferences to a situation. Deductive reasoning guarantees the truth of the conclusion, whereas inductive reasoning does not provide absolute assurance. Deductive reasoning is common in mathematics and logic. Inductive reasoning is common in science and social affairs. Computers can fine-tune options and alternatives to ensure accuracy.

AI provides amazing capabilities and results. It is used in Alexa, Siri, and Netflix. But more importantly, various AI is applied in medicine, manufacturing, finance, retail, transportation, education, and the military. Many project that AI may eventually duplicate human intelligence.

According to Raj Reddy, there are "about 100 million neural cells in the human brain and might be performing 200 trillion operations per second if not faster than that."[13] Humans can also think with images, which is far different than step-by-step reasoning.

AI expert systems can do some things the human mind is unable to do. They provide permanent storage for information and knowledge for consultation and serve as a depository of expert sources and storehouse of knowledge.

Intelligence has several dimensions. Based on Robert Sternberg's[14] research, there are three aspects to it for success in life. One is analytical intelligence, which is analyzing and evaluating problems and determining solutions. Basically, this is what IQ tests measure. Another aspect is creative intelligence, which institutes novel and interesting ideas along with problem solving and innovation in order to solve problems.

Practical intelligence is another category that involves the ability to confront problems in life and discern the best fit between themselves and the demands of the context and environment. Using knowledge from experience, changing, and adapting to circumstances by alters the environment or creates a new one.

NOTES

1. Edward-Isaac Dovere, "The Pull of Andrew Yang's Pessimism," *The Atlantic*, August 15, 2019.

2. Frontline, "In the Age of AI," *Public Broadcasting System*, Season 38, Episode 5, November 5, 2019, https://www.pbs.org/wgbh/frontline/film/in-the-age-of-ai/.

3. John Gardner, *Frames of Mind* (New York: Basic Books, 1985).

4. John Gardner, *Five Minds for the Future* (Boston, MA: Harvard Business Press, 2008), 154–58.

5. Alexander Ruchti, "The Ups and Downs of Artificial Intelligence," September 15, 2019, https://www.juliusbaer.com/en/insights/artificial-intelligence/the-ups-and-downs-of-artificial-intelligence/.

6. John McCarthy, Marvin L. Minsky, Nathaniel Rochester, and Claude E. Shannon, "A Proposal for the Dartmouth Research Project on Artificial Intelligence," *AI Magazine* 27, no. 4 (2006).

7. Brian McGuire, *The History of Artificial Intelligence* (University of Washington, December 2006), 4

8. Frontline, 2.

9. John D. Kelleher, *Deep Learning* (Cambridge, MA: The MIT Press, 2019), 11.

10. Delotte, Artificial Intelligence Defined, March 2018, https://www2.deloitte.com/content/dam/Deloitte/nl/Documents/deloitte-analytics/deloitte-nl-data-analytics-artificial-intelligence-whitepaper-eng.pdf.

11. New Generation Applications, https://www.newgenapps.com/blog/3-levels-of-artificial-intelligence/.

12. Artificial Intelligence, https://www.britanica.com.

13. Ting Huang, "Expert Systems," *The History of Artificial Intelligence* (University of Washington, 2006), 15.

14. Charlotte Ruhl, "Intelligence: Definition, Theories, and Testing," *Simply Psychology*, July 16, 2020, https://www.simplypsychology.org/intelligence.html.

Chapter 6

From Butterflies to Black Swans

Technology progression and advancement has always been met with fear and anxiety, giving way to tremendous gains for humankind as we learn to enhance the best of the changes and adapt and alter the worst.

—David Wells, Former CEO, Netflix

People plan to reach goals and dreams they have for a happy life. Plans, however, do not always work and some go adrift, circumvented by chance and small, unexpected, and seemingly inconsequential events. Life involves butterflies, but also an occasional Black Swan.

The butterfly effect, discussed earlier, involves the circumstances when one small change, metaphorically the flapping of a butterfly's wings, creates huge events and consequences. Small changes, in other words, can generate massive effects.

Where do Black Swans come into the picture? Black Swan theory is a metaphor for unexpected events unfurled surprisingly with a major influence beyond normal expectation. In ancient times, Black Swans were thought not to exist. Improbabilities do occur, and outliers to contemporary thought occur, carrying an extreme impact. Black Swans are difficult to predict because of their rarity: individuals recognize them only in retrospect. For example, the September 11, 2001, terrorist attack in New York City was an unforeseen incursion. People generally recognize the result only in hindsight.

The COVID-19 pandemic created an unforeseen lockdown of the United States and the world economically, socially, and educationally and in terms of entertainment and commerce. Individuals had to stay home from work, family, and other responsibilities. Medical facilities struggled with the demand and services and vaccine.

Atypical events are hard to predict and go beyond the normal parameters of past history. Rare events such as this shifted perspective as people experienced emotion and apprehension that were not previously of great concern or even possible. Sometimes the perception and biases of people blind them to the possible repercussions of events, as well as how to progress through them.

A shift, however, is not necessarily a change or certainly not a transformation. With such events or a crisis, the expectation is that once it is solved things will go back to "normal." Events are seen as a blip on the radar.

Shifts basically involve a slight move in position or direction or an adjustment: putting some things aside and replacing them with others. For example, a shift is working from home in the same job rather than having to go to the office—responsibilities and duties remain the same, but where and how the work is completed is not.

Change, on the other hand, converts something or alters its course and focus, incrementally and unexpectedly—totally unplanned because of unforeseen circumstances, emergencies, or conditions. Or, change can also be transitional, achieving the same desired state through a different strategy, operation, or resource. Some of these conditions and requirements can be stressful, caused by a perceived loss of control or aspirations.

Transformation, however, is much deeper and complex because it is a metamorphosis into a complete alteration from one thing into another. It is a major alteration in form, purpose, function, or nature. In business, some companies transform from one focus to another. IBM, for example, transformed from a company selling low-margin PCs, computer chips, and hardware to providing expertise on information technology and computing services to businesses.

Transformation creates levels of insecurity socially, economically, and personally because individuals perceive their lives becoming disoriented and challenged. Present levels of status and living standards come into question. Greater inequalities arise when jobs may require new skills and education, training, and location. This could have a greater effect on older employees. Adapting to circumstances takes time, which may involve short-term losses before achieving any long-term gain. Time is necessary because the total effect of transformations and resolution becomes clear slowly.

All individuals experience shifts and change; they are normal aspects of growing through life, relationships and experience, and successes and failures. People must adapt to the greater responsibilities of adulthood, the requirements and pressures of careers and family life, as well as the transitional phases of life from childhood to old age. These transformations are not new or unique: every person has experienced them to some degree.

In conflict, individuals sometimes say, "This is not the world I live in." Basically, how they see the world is a product of their experiences and perceptions—the depiction and expectation in their minds about the world they live in and how it should work.

People seldom think about how they think. The Irish poet and writer John O'Donohue wrote, "When you become aware of your thoughts and your particular style of thinking, you begin to see why your world is shaped the way it is."[1] The world, however, may not operate in line with one's perspective.

In transformational times, however, an established or rigid mindset can be problematic. The world, as they perceive it, may be long gone because transformations and the forces at work altered social, economic, and other aspects of life. How people comprehend and think is challenged, and their lens on the future and its possibilities can be frozen and out of line with a clear picture of reality.

Uncertainty is difficult and the unknown is frightening, particularly when important aspects of life are directly influenced. People become prisoners of their own thoughts and their approach or style of thinking, which restricts creativity and imagination and limits thinking anew and in fresh ways. Progress can be painful. With uncertainty about gains and losses, there are real and imagined fears. Past history highlights some areas to observe. Daily life, education, and communication are certainly affected. In addition, the economic consequences are vital and often unclear for workers of all kinds, whether labor, skilled, or professional. Family life's comfort and future become at risk.

All transformational times produce unpredictability and risk. Questions about today and certainly tomorrow are present, many of which are not clearly answerable. "What about my kids' future?" "What about my job?" "What's the economic impact of this transformation?" "Will life have the same depth of meaning for me?" "Why is this happening?" "Will I be useless to my family?" "What can I do?"

Unemployment, underemployment, and intermittent employment are always worries for men and women who care for their families and futures. The impact on the elderly and youth is not always clear because transformation does not flow equally as it promotes and launches unanticipated changes and reforms in various areas and fields. It also can push changes and reforms as other creative ideas are nurtured through the application and impact of reform.

A new era approaches with automation and machines that we think will influence people's daily lives and also future successes and purpose. Technological change—particularly artificial intelligence—is commanding and pervasive. The total consequences are unclear, which raises doubt and concern.

The press and social and political leaders tout the positive prospects of artificial intelligence. While some positives are evident, there are also downsides to any transformation, including artificial intelligence. The Industrial Age and the Age of the Knowledge Worker had both merits for many and serious issues for others. The concern is that some results are clear, others are speculative, and, of course, others are total unknowns.

KNOWNS AND UNKNOWNS

With any transformation, speculation abounds on both sides of the aisle—supporters and pessimists. The truth is as things evolve there are hypotheses, some accurate and others pure conjecture.

Former Secretary of Defense Donald Rumsfeld famously stated: "there are known knowns; there are things we know we know. We also know there are known unknowns; that is to say we know there are some things we do not know. But there are also unknown unknowns—the ones we don't know we don't know. And if one looks throughout the history of our country and other free countries, it is the latter category that tend to be the difficult ones."[2]

Businesses and government have confronted the "unknown unknowns" dilemma, which requires taking all forms of knowledge into account with an open mind. AI can make predictions based on data analysis. However, "unknown unknowns" may exist, but data may be void of any sense, intuitive or otherwise, of the possibilities taking shape. Data is one thing, however, philosophical commitment and values and other intangibles cannot be expressed mathematically.

This is especially true concerning transformations. Not all of the positives and negatives are foreseen. Advocates visualize what artificial intelligence brings to individuals as well as the economy and society. Some positives become obvious in time as the application of artificial intelligence is applied possibly in ways that were unforeseen.

On the other side of the ledger, there are downsides. No idea or concept has only upsides. Gains sometimes come with losses, and to ignore those possibilities can be dangerous or contrary to applying proper values and principles. Learning from past transformations demonstrates, among other things, that they come with positive and negative implications and complications, both short-term and long-term.

John Bilden in his article on the unknown unknowns of intellectual technology indicated that poor estimates are a result of unknown unknowns.[3] He believes that discovering "unknown unknowns" could be understood by asking several questions to ensure greater accuracy of estimates. They include:

- Is there a fundamental understanding of the case for change and a clear definition of the capabilities required for transformation?

- What are the consequences of deployment (of the technology)? What is the expected decision model—the amount of participation expected to support the transformation: deployment, training, support, etc.?
- What level of talent is required to achieve productivity and other goals?

Government and business transformation fails based on these and other issues. Citizens, however, do not have detailed data or information to understand what is totally happening. Progress and change can be difficult and painful; and unknowns create uncertainty and alarm.

With change and certainly transformation, anxiety exists in many aspects of a person's life. Looking back in time during prior historical transformations, some individuals benefited greatly from them and others not. Simply put, winners and losers! The universal question before full implementation is: who gains and who does not from a personal and business standpoint?

Gaining an understanding of the nature and implications of transformations is necessary for citizens to look to the future. Not an easy thing. First of all, the average citizen may not have any general or accurate information about what is unfolding and why. Even scientists do not comprehend every effect for citizens in all demographic groups. Remember the unknown unknowns.

Innovation and transformation are not socially or economically neutral. Not only are there economic and employment concerns but there are others as well. Consequences involve political and other principles and values. There are nonmaterial impacts of reform: attitudes can change and commitments increase or waiver. In addition, ethical and moral questions also raise major concerns.

During these periods, contentment and satisfaction are at risk. The "old days" were not necessarily exemplary, but they were experienced and understood. Turning the corner into a transforming culture does not happen quickly and is an ongoing process. What brought satisfaction in the past may be harder to encounter in the future.

Speech and Privacy

Certainly with the present and future growth of artificial intelligence, social concerns of civil rights and individual freedoms are raised. The impact of the Internet has affected the nature and freedom of expression. Freedom of speech and the right of free expression can be at risk through censorship and cancellation of opinions by social and political groups and others. The concept of hate speech is already in play and some individuals have lost their jobs or positions because of the characterization of their written or verbal comments or opinions. Some have had their messages censored and labeled negatively by others.

The basic right is freedom of speech. Today a vast majority is done through technology and Internet. What is popular may not be correct, and what is unpopular may be correct. What is civil or uncivil is open to individual judgment many times. Legally, however, court opinions on free speech concluded that yelling "fire" in a crowded theater presents a physical danger to others and can be legally restricted speech.

As part of limiting discussion, censoring and labeling others through epithets and derision is frequently used. Censorship and freedom of speech have been consistent issues in all democracies. What are the criteria and who or what agency decides when censorship is the correct pathway?

According to the American Civil Liberties Union, there are only two fundamental principles that affect freedom of speech. One is that the government cannot limit free expression of content just because any listener, or even the majority of a community, is offended. In art and entertainment, people have to accept works they find offensive or outrageous. Second, expression may only be restricted if it clearly causes direct and imminent harm to important societal interests—falsely shouting "fire" in a crowded theater.

Privacy is also critically important to a democracy and to individual lives. Concerns have been expressed that citizens and organizations are having their personal or business email, telephone, and fiscal accounts "hacked." In a sense, technology has made some people more vulnerable concerning privacy and their reputation.

In addition, the prevalence of cameras and facial identification is concerning on two fronts—accuracy and privacy. Should the government be able to invade your privacy when out socially or for business? The research indicates that camera identification of individual spaces is not without accuracy problems. Does this raise the specter that "Big Brother" is watching you?

Transformation affects an individuals' identities: their manner of perceiving and thinking about themselves and their environment. What should people do in light of events and transformation is a dramatic question. Transformation is out of any individuals' control and the feeling of victimization can arise. Feeling oppressed or endangered is possible. Actions and reactions are unclear. A broad view of what is occurring is not easy to perceive. Individuals' intelligence and problem-solving abilities may be restrained, while further economic and social well-being and autonomy are seemingly compromised.

In these times, people still feel emotionally tied to what they know and experienced. The feeling of personal loss causes individuals to have a sense of denial and anger and is emotionally depressing. Moving to a sense of acceptance requires exploring how to adjust to this new time, as well as finding support from others to move ahead and adapt to life-altering times.

Citizens must understand the ethical and moral implications in the application and use of transformational technology and other innovations.

Happiness

Personal happiness, as a consequence, is at risk. Unfamiliar settings and perceived alienating surroundings create a sense of distress, heartbreak, and insecurity. Anxiety and apprehension curtail a positive point of view, as individuals perceive the best of their lives evaporating. The prospect of a darker future is disquieting. The concern or appearance of fragmentation and exposure of individual lives creates conflict and social concerns.

Times of transformation bring fundamental questions. Not everything that matters is tangible or material. Having an abundance of fame, money, and expensive things does not bring happiness. Material comfort after a while loses its luster. Feeling good from golfing or buying a new car, for example, is not identical with happiness. Feeling good and happiness are not synonymous.

Martin Seligman, in his book *Flourish*,[4] indicated that authentic happiness has three elements. First, positive emotion; what people feel is important. "Pleasure, rapture, ecstasy, warmth, comfort, are significant to a "pleasant life."

A second element is flow, which involves "being one with the music, time stopping, in the loss of self-consciousness during an absorbing activity." Individuals become merged with the activity, which absorbs both thought and feeling. Basically, the colloquialism, of being in the "zone," fully immersed and focused. This entails cognitive and emotional concentration.

The third element is extremely important in all times, particularly during transformations. Finding meaning! Pursuing pleasure is one thing, but finding meaning is essential. People want and need meaning in their lives, not simply the pursuit of pleasure.

Individuals want meaning in their lives, having a purpose beyond self, and contributing to important concerns and values. A meaningful life consists of serving and belonging to something bigger than oneself—family, religion, political principles, and others. Finding a mission and pursuing a cause is important and more than "stardom." Basically, significance rests on relationships (love/forgiveness), meaning, and self-contentment.

History illustrates that the commitment of values and principles is necessary. Beliefs and a higher mission in life make family and neighborhoods better, through sacrifice, time, and energy for the greater good, which has a far deeper meaning than strictly self-interest.

Transformational times raise the specter that these elements of meaning may be blocked, and the ability to pursue them will be lost and sacrificed in a new era. Meaningful work contributions and ensuring one's talents and abilities lead to a life of consequence and happiness.

Too often leaders and others discount happiness as an issue. Fearing the loss of contributing and pursuing one's talents and interests is certainly raised with the specter of artificial intelligence and technology. Some feel they will be replaced, become meaningless, and their lives altered without recourse. Everything seems beyond their control.

Technology has moved in spurts over the last seventy-five years. Now it is more available and projected to have an even larger and dramatic impact on all aspects of economic and private social life. These impacts also carry major concerns in how people perceive their life and future.

NOTES

1. John O'Donohue, *Eternal Echoes* (New York: Cliff Street Books, 1999), 94.

2. Defense.gov News Transcript: DoD News Briefing—Sec. Rumsfeld and Gen. Myers, United States Department of Defense, February 12, 2002.

3. John Belden, "Exploring the 'Unknown Unknowns' in IT," *CIO*, December 14, 2018.

4. E. P. Martin Seligman, *Flourish: A Visionary New Understanding of Happiness and Well-Being* (Atria Books, 2011), Kindle edition, 11–12.

Chapter 7

Artificial Intelligence

Real World Issues

Success in creating artificial intelligence would be the biggest event in human history. Unfortunately, it might be the last, unless we learn how to avoid the risks.

—Stephen Hawking, Physicist

Artificial intelligence doesn't have to be able to destroy humanity—if artificial intelligence has a goal and humanity just happens in the way, it will destroy humanity as a matter of course without even thinking about it, no hard feelings.

—Elon Musk, Technology Entrepreneur

How any technology, like artificial intelligence, is applied today and in the future is not always clearly evident. Optimists look to the heavens and pessimists see darkness. The power of innovation is not always clear and it comes with consequences, both obvious and subtle. The fate was always in the hands of humans. Artificial intelligence brings amazing capability and data management and analysis but also opens doors you could only imagine. Technology that could think independently was far beyond anyone's perceived reality.

Thinking machines bring new horizons because they can direct or make decisions, which can be independent of human influence. If that is the case, what is required of the individuals and organizations involved in its application? Thinking technology needs limits and control—limits on content and actions exist for individuals based on law and moral standards. People also have self-control based on conscience, ethics, and values that direct their decisions, particularly in new, difficult, or unclear times. They have emotions and analytical and evaluative thinking skills and understand philosophical questions concerning individuals and societal integrity.

The general public is becoming more aware of the progression of technology and employment. According to a PEW[1] study, 54 percent of workers perceive continuous training as essential and another 33 percent perceive it to be important, but not essential. Concerning skills, 83 percent indicate social skills are required, and 77 percent designate the importance and necessity of analytical skills. Only 18 percent stated that physical skills are essential.

In society today, conjecture and projections create speculation and suppositions that may not be valid or possible. As in all professions and businesses there are subjects and factors seemingly irrelevant that grow into principled, major questions. The controlling forces in these situations are ethics and values that provide guidance.

Observations about the consequences of technology are both concerning and optimistic. In another survey, PEW found that with American adults:[2]

- Seventy-two percent are worried about robots and computers doing human jobs. But 33 percent are enthusiastic.
- Sixty-seven percent believe that artificial intelligence algorithms will evaluate and hire job candidates, while 22 percent do not.
- Fifty-four percent versus 40 percent believe in the development of driverless vehicles.

Economic innovations result in financial concerns. Unspoken fears and emotional loss carry not only tangible physical but also psychological pressure. Making a living for family and self carries heavy and deep responsibilities. Losing a job brings concrete hardships and worries about the present as well as the future. Some individuals may find comparable jobs with other employers. Others discover it very difficult to gain employment in equivalent roles. Incomes suffer but so do individuals' personal and physical lives.

Artificial intelligence will eliminate many jobs dealing with routine work. However, roles requiring people skills, such as listening and empathy, are not currently the province of technology, even thinking machines. A computer or robot will not replace kindergarten teachers or people in similar roles that require transmitting caring, understanding, and emotional support, affection, and active listening.

Many people perceive technology as strictly related to mathematics and science, causing reticence or trepidation for some in using it. The application of algorithms is not always evident to individuals: some technological terminology is alien to some citizens and sounds complex and beyond their scope. Jargon can be unnerving and create misunderstanding.

The RAND Corporation in a research brief, "The Future of Work—Trends and Implications," stated that employees will work in "more decentralized, specialized firms" and that "greater emphasis will be placed on retraining and lifelong learning."[3] RAND specifies that workforces will have to adapt to technology and the shifts in product demands. Knowledge-based work requires cognitive skills such as abstract reasoning, problem solving, collaboration, and communication. Technological sophistication and prominence will require a higher skilled workforce.

MACHINE LEARNING

Machine learning for technology is not the same as artificial intelligence. "Artificial intelligence is usually a broad concept of machines being smart. In other words, it is the science behind intelligent computers. On the other hand, machine learning is a technology used to teach machines to access data and learn for themselves."[4]

SAS,[5] a leading analytics company in artificial intelligence, has machine learning, which is a method of data analysis based on the concept that the system can "learn" from data, define patterns, and make decisions with minimal human intervention.

While machine learning is possible there are certain jobs they will not take over—even smart machines. Inventors, for example, because the work requires thinking outside the box, not always in linear thought patterns and are not governed by defined rules, insights, or processes. Creativity does not rely on established perspectives.

The development of technology and its application is constantly evolving, with different and increasing levels of technological capabilities. Artificial technology involves machines that can learn from experience. The AlphaGo example, along with computers that can be trained to process large portfolios of data, can recognize patterns and project issues and strategies.

Another aspect is Deep Learning, which trains a computer to perform human-like tasks like recognizing speech, identifying images, and making predictions. Deep Learning establishes the basic parameters about the data and trains the computer to learn on its own to recognize patterns.

Artificial intelligence also helps computers understand and interpret human language—natural language processing (NLP). NLP helps computers and humans to communicate in human language, which allows computers to read text, hear speech, and interpret it.

Another aspect of life and communication is vision. Computer vision in artificial intelligence trains the computer to interpret and form a mental image of the world. With digital camera images and videos, along with Deep Learning, computers can identify and classify objects and people. For example, being able to identify an image of a cat without any label and to differentiate between a cat and a chair.[6] Technology that is able to differentiate and define things in pictures is a broad step.

All artificial intelligence is not the same: there are different degrees of intelligence and purpose. Basically, several types of artificial intelligence exist for business: automating business processes, data analysis, evaluation, and engagement with workers and customers.

Process automation involves digital and physical tasks: back-office and financial activities such as transforming data from email and call centers into systems of record. Additionally, replacing lost credit cards and updating records, reading legal or contract documents, and extracting provisions in natural language processing are completed.[7] Robotic processing is the easiest to apply.

Cognitive insight is another aspect of artificial intelligence in which algorithms detect patterns in vast volumes of data and interpret their meaning. For example, cognitive insight is used to predict what a particular customer will buy, identify fraud in real time, and automate personalized targeting of digital ads.

Cognitive insight is data intensive, detailed, and applied to make predictions. Some versions of deep learning machines can recognize images and speech. These applications do not generally threaten human jobs because they involve high-speed data crunching and analysis beyond timely human capability.

Another technology is cognitive engagement that connects customers and employees using natural language. It is the least common—16 percent of the total. This involves technological interactions with people in order to answer frequently asked questions. Chatbots are used to conduct conversations via text or audio and they operate either under simple predefined rules or through the use of artificial intelligence. Both can increase the speed of communication and response time between customers and the agents of organizations.

Cognitive engagement answers questions through information technology about employee benefits or policy. Recommendation systems are used to provide and create customized care plans taking into account an individual's health status and previous treatment.

Artificial intelligence, however, cannot do some things humans can. For example, it cannot read the way humans do because it cannot understand concepts like time, place, or causality.[8] In addition, it does not have emotional intelligence, which humans use to interpret and comprehend what they are reading, hearing, or observing. Satire or sarcasm could be a mystery for artificial intelligence.

BUSINESSES AND EMPLOYMENT

To be competitive in a market-driven economy change is inevitable. New products. Efficiencies. Innovation. Technology. All have an impact on production, customer service, and quality. The market is highly competitive and employees must make decisions necessary to remain in business and to invest in facilities, equipment, service, and talent. Politicians speak about creating jobs, but they better examine science and technology and understand the increasing impact of artificial intelligence and the nature of the future workforce.

Technology will and has brought challenges for both employers and employees. There certainly are benefits to business. In a survey of 250 executives, they indicated that they wanted to make products better: 51 percent cited enhancing the future functions and performance of their products as a primary reason.[9] In addition, 36 percent cited that technology freed up workers to be more creative through automation of tasks and improved decision making.

Artificial intelligence is one of the most important technologies to come to prominence and encourages and supports the development of others. Technology creates efficiency that reduces costs, resource allocation, management, and increases information efficiencies that impact employment.

Changes in technology and business models make some roles and jobs obsolete. While innovation has an effect on markets and lifestyle, it also comes with social and economic costs on individuals and businesses. These are difficult conversions and challenges. An extreme example is the bankruptcy of Kodak, the creator of the digital camera. At its highest point, it employed 145,300 people. With the emergence of Instagram, Kodak in 2012 was declared bankrupt.

Almost half of the executives cited the difficulty of integrating cognitive projects with existing processes and systems.[10] Thirty-seven percent indicated that managers do not understand cognitive technologies and how they work. Another issue raised by 40 percent of the executives was the expense of technology and the expertise necessary to operate it, and 35 percent stated that they could not find enough people with technological expertise.

A major success factor is people's willingness to learn. Some are eager to discover new approaches and others want to stick with the tools with which they are familiar. Americans think that in fifty years, it is likely that computers and robots will do all of the work.

HUMAN ADVANTAGES

Human beings have some distinct advantages over artificial intelligence. For one, they have diverse senses—eyes, ears, smell, and touch. Personality and character are essential in building effective organizations. In communication, emotional feelings involve more than simply saying and defining words. Determining intent of words and communication are essential in interpreting content; data and metrics cannot always measure subtle and intangible influences such as moods, emotion, and memories.

Judgment and understanding philosophical principles are key factors in hiring. Judgment can make or break data, decisions, and efforts. Decisions are complex and sometimes relatively small factors create large consequences. Judgment and qualitative understanding rests on experience, perception, and emotional context. The cornerstone of judgment and decisions is philosophical principles and values. Relationships move beyond skills.

Predictions are not easy because of the risk of success and high reward versus loss and failure. Not all factors and circumstances are equal, tangible, and metrically measurable. Individuals get married on the basis of emotion—love. The impact of emotion is not quantifiable and its impact and intensity is different for each person. Emotion and beliefs compose the essence of working relationships for teams. What metric could people rely on to determine whether or not they want a close relationship with a particular person? Metrics have no impact, while love and connection are necessary for success.

ATTITUDES AND PERSPECTIVE

Times of uncertainty and dramatic change create several possibilities in people's minds. Without concrete information, clarification is not available and they look at the future with "uninformed optimism."[11] This simply means that they don't know exactly how their life will evolve, but they feel they can imagine it. Others, however, see it differently.

As change progresses and realities become evident, individuals may move to "informed pessimism." In this case, they realize and experience how change will affect them and recognize tangible and intangible consequences. They check out the questions and challenges and realize the concerns they have for their future and families.

A next phase is "hopeful realism" in which people feel they can adapt and move through the process. The final stage is "informal optimism" in which pessimism decreases and they feel confidence in moving through a new way of life.

Several trends, according to the RAND Corporation,[12] are evident in times of transformation in light of the fact that firms are becoming more specialized and outsource "non-core" functions. RAND speculates that there will be a shift from "more permanent lifetime jobs toward less permanent even nonstandard employment relationships"—self-employed, distance work.

People will work in decentralized firms and relationships will be more individualized and less standardized. The context will emphasize retraining and lifelong learning so companies can remain competitive in a global market. As a result, growth and productivity will support raising wages and altered wage distribution. Access to fringe benefits will be more limited.

The growth of knowledge-based work also favors non-routine cognitive skills and abstract reasoning, problem solving, communication, and collaboration, some of which may be done with artificial intelligence. Obviously, a deep understanding of computer technology and its use is necessary. Higher levels of social and analytical skills are required for higher paying jobs. Jobs will change as automation complements people in their roles.

Machine learning requires access to data and artificial intelligence in order for the system to have the ability to automatically learn and improve. It requires access to computer programs, data, and information. The potential of artificial intelligence in white-collar and other more complicated roles can enable those with disabilities greater opportunity.

On the horizon, the potential of artificial intelligence to complete tasks and the growth and its ability to "learn" will have great impact—not only in innovations but also in being able to develop self-supervised learning in technology. Self-supervised learning involves artificial intelligence being able to train itself without the need for external labels attached to the data.

As artificial intelligence expands, it will impact a vast number of occupations and organizations. Issues will be raised with concerns about employment, but also education, security, and ethics. Transformation and reform create significant modifications in many aspects of culture, economy, and employment. Leadership is necessary.

NOTES

1. PEW Research, "The State of American Jobs," https://pewsocialtrends.org/2016/10/06/the-state-of-American-jobs

2. PEW Research, "Automation in Everyday Life," https://pewresaerch.org.intenet/2017/10/04/automation-in-everyday-life.

3. RAND Corporation, "The Future of Work—Trends and Implications," https://www.rand.org/pubs/research_briefs/RB5070.html.

4. Chris Baker, A*rtificial Intelligence—A Modern Approach* (Kindle edition, 2019), 43.

5. SAS, "Five AI Technologies That You Need to Know," https://www.sas.com/en_us/insights/articles/analytics/five-ai-technologies.html.

6. Stephen Rosenbush, "Facebook's AI Chief Pushes the Technologies Limits," *Wall Street Journal*, August 13, 2020.

7. Thomas Davenport, and Rajeev Ronanki, "AI for the Real World," *Harvard Business Review*, January–February 2008.

8. Lasse Rouhiornen, "Artificial Intelligence: 101 Things You Must No Today About Our Future," Kindle edition, 2018, 18.

9. Davenport and Ronanki, "AI for the Real World."

10. PEW Research Center, "Public Predictions for the Future and Workforce Automation," https://www.pewresearch.org/internet/2016/03/10/public-predictions-for-the-future-of-workforce-automation/.

11. Minnesota State Employee Assistance Program, "Ups and Downs for Layoff Survivors," https://mn.gov/mmb/assets/ups-downs.pdf0_tcm1059-130193.pdf.

12. RAND Corporation, "The Future of Work."

Chapter 8

Gains and Concerns

In order for AI technologies to be truly transformative in a positive way, we need a set of ethical norms, standards, and practical mythologies to ensure that we use AI responsibly and to the benefit of humanity.

—Susan Etlinger

ANALYST: DATA AND DIGITAL STRATEGY

Liberty, free speech, inalienable rights, and responsibility have defined Americans. The assumption is that people have the ability to engage in self-government. Totalitarian regimes are the opposite. Free thought is destroyed and individuals must fall into line and adopt dictated speech and principles and follow the directed course and rules.

In the seventeenth and eighteenth centuries principles about the importance of people and free will establish the framework for contemporary society. Philosophically, countries like the United States encapsulated those ideas and principles in their founding documents and culture.

Americans have traditionally been described as autonomous individuals, who think for themselves. They are not sheep and are willing to stand alone. Today, however, people may be more automated than they surmise. In many aspects of life, they are following recommendations and decisions by algorithms.

Technology affects people's perception of reality. Certainly, it has influenced the analysis and presentations of material. Polls and their metrical "analyses" are constantly published. Some individuals feel that numbers are free of bias or distortion. If it is a metric, it must be factual because numbers do not lie. But they can. How they are collected and analyzed matters: sample size, database, the manner in which the questions are stated, the expertise of the responders, and other issues affect the credibility of the comments and their conclusions. What is fact or fiction is an issue users must discern—what is behind the matrix and the reliability and truthfulness of the conclusions?

Numbers do not always illustrate or define reality, nor are they always synonymous with truth. The technology in use today has issues that "include dealing with inconsistent and incomplete knowledge, individualizing systems to the needs of particular users, fostering collaborative interaction, planning under resource constraints, tracking change in users and systems, dealing with plain old heart-to-heart every day 'naïve' users (rather than 'helpful' or 'expert' users), making systems easy to use, developing and managing distributed and fragmented software systems."[1]

Algorithms are not genius or magical or beyond human understanding. They are written and reviewed by humans, and they are not free of biases toward segments of society or philosophical or political positions. Experts have raised concerns that people defer to technology and data because they think it is objective and free of passion or prejudice, because numbers and data analysis appear to be objective and logical. But there are big risks.

Algorithms are subject to GIGO: garbage in, garbage out. This simply means that the output of any algorithm is only as good as the quality of the input. Technology does not solve the issue of bias and truth as some think. Machine learning can be just as skewed and subjective as the perspective of human beings. After all, they wrote and determined what data was to be used in them.

Artificial intelligence offers some obvious positives. Besides efficiency, it can provide data and information that is easily available, as well as managing resources like finances, energy, and others. But there are questions about artificial intelligence and the possibility and ability to think.

Today, people experience totally routine and automated customer service. This is only going to expand as companies and institutions move to widespread adoption.

The implementation of more powerful artificial intelligence takes time, money, and training because it involves entire companies and employees across functions, which raises different perspectives and skill requirements. Addressing employee uncertainty and apprehension is necessary.

Staff throughout the hierarchy need to understand how artificial intelligence affects the decision-making process. In some cases, for example, technology is solely capable of making simple and routine decisions. However, artificial intelligence in its deeper levels makes suggestions or decisions independently or in partnership with human beings. The "algorithm's recommendations can arrive at better answers than either humans or machines could reach on their own."[2] But there are concerns.

People have to cautiously trust the algorithms' recommendation. But this trust comes with a potential glitch—Algorithms, themselves! They direct artificial intelligence through a set of instructions designed to perform a specific task. It can be as simple as multiplying two numbers or as complex an operation based on the sequence of well-defined, multifaceted computer instructions. Algorithms are designed to get a specific output through logical, coherent, and pertinent programming steps.

Citizens and employers need to understand how technology and humans make judgments. All judgments have consequences and depend on accurate and unbiased information. Human decisions are made hopefully on knowledge and principles.

In many cases, bias is not intentional: it can be through program design, testing, or application of databases.[3] Concerning design, biases can be in the selection of the training data set and the training itself. Because of past biases and history of society, data can be indicative of various gender, race, and political or other prejudices. Data can be collected at times when social values and prejudices affected how it was collected. Biases against gender, race, ethnic, or other factors can be a factor in the times data were collected, where and how it was gathered, and by whom.

Consequently, flawed or limited data can result in bias. This is no different an issue than the judgment of human beings who apply flawed facts, personal preferences, or incomplete and inaccurate data to make decisions.

The analytic structure and data sources for the algorithms may not be credible. Many individuals do not question metrics or the results because they do not understand research, data sources, and how data was analyzed and interpreted. They believe that numbers and their mathematical analyses must be true—numbers, however, may not clearly define issues and the intangibles that go with them.

Another issue not easily evident is "what data was left out" and not considered. In presidential races, the polls were not accurate during the campaign process or outcome. Pollsters' projections are based on sample characteristics, size, and diversity.

Were polls inaccurate because of how they were designed and implemented? Who was and was not included in the size of samples or other factors? Because of the political atmosphere and undertone of the election debates and media, many did not trust the pollsters and did not report their opinions honestly. Were the poll questions clear and unbiased? Wording of questions is important to get accurate answers.

What is being measured and assessed is another issue. The development of the algorithms is a crucial step in this process. "If we choose to measure that which is easy to measure—or easier to measure—and not think through the unintended consequences and struggle with measuring messier things, we can come up with very clean, beautiful algorithmic solutions, but we run the risk of exacerbating the equity issues."[4]

The algorithms must be open to review to ensure that the result will not be tainted and that there are no blind spots in the research.

Data must accurately represent the issue at hand and the population and context; otherwise it results in selection bias. For example, in a past machine-learning model, the words female and women were correlated with pursuits like homemaking and the arts, and the words male or man were tagged to engineering and mathematics.[5] While not formulated purposely, prejudice based on preconceived gender roles was the result.

Concerns exist about artificial intelligence–based recommendations and the databases from which they are made. Just because it comes in the form of a research project does not mean it is totally factual or unbiased. The algorithm and database are major concerns in decisions made through algorithmic data analysis. Numbers and data are not free of potential bias. What organization completed the research is also a factor in its goals and on how it was completed. Special interests exist in business, political, academic, and other organizations that have positions and objectives that are in their interests. Understanding the results of interest groups must be reviewed and analyzed for accuracy and clarity. Too frequently groups will indicate "research shows" without independent parties having any ability to review the research or its conclusions.

Algorithms

Algorithms are at the essence of artificial intelligence. They are at the core of how artificial intelligence works and the product it produces. Many individuals do not understand them and how they function. Because they utilize so-called hard data, people think they are accurate and free of any bias or error. But that is not the case. Like all systems, technology and data can have biases and significant issues.

The nature of the algorithm, the procedural steps, and the data are essential to the quality of the outcome. Analytics are at the core of data-based decisions, which raises two issues. First, do metrical data provide an accurate and comprehensive analysis of the situation or circumstances? Are there nonmeasurable influences that shaped the issue beyond what is metrically measurable in the database? Are emotions or unforeseen or intangible forces influential that are not contained in the data?

Secondly, are there biases in the algorithm or database that add prejudice to the outcome? Was all the essential data in the database? What was not evident? Biases can be in the data itself because of when and who collected and managed it. Was the data comprehensive or limited? Was a sample size of the data appropriate? Are there any biases in the database on gender, race, age, education, religion, or any other factor? The analyses are only as good as the quality of the algorithm and database.

Research is only valid if it is the result of well-constructed and defined plans. Violating any of the guides for valid research will make it unreliable. Research bias includes:

1. Asking wrong questions: questions that do not capture the full scope of the survey's issue.
2. Surveying the wrong people: researchers must target the population that fits the goals of the survey. Clarity of the population for the research is extremely important.
3. Collection methods: survey methods must ensure that people can take part in the survey. People with specific expertise may be required in a study, not the general public. Just surveying people walking down the street is not a guaranteed representative sample.
4. Misinterpreting data results: basically this is misinterpreting raw data by using inaccurate or inappropriate statistical techniques, which will not interpret the raw data correctly: excellent data and poor statistical analysis result in erroneous conclusions.

Below are measurement errors that can be present in data collection and analysis. In examining so-called research assessment procedures, reviewing these five categories is appropriate.

- Sampling error: occurs in a statistical analysis arising from the under-representativeness of the sample taken. The sample is inaccurate or too small for the population studied or for the numbers of individuals collected for study.
- Measurement error: created when the questions are confusing and the respondents respond based on the confusion. Posing questions, wording of questionnaires, or the way the data were collected must be clear.
- Selection bias: the sample should be randomly selected, otherwise biases can occur that distort the concept of randomness. Correct procedures are necessary to ensure the sample rendered is random for the population studied.
- No response bias: this occurs when some people fail to respond to the survey or interview. Sometimes, the nature and topic of this survey will repel individuals from participating, for example, cheating on taxes, alcoholism, or sexual conduct. How the data is obtained also can affect responses. Collecting survey data on cell phones may attract younger persons but destroys the concept of a random sample across population groups.

- Voluntary response bias: some surveys are designed to attract opinion-ated people. Radio shows are good examples. Under-representation is a problem in the so-called surveys because it's not a random sample but one motivated because of political or other reasons.

With any database or artificial intelligence program, the outputs are only as good as the algorithms, data, and input. Technology is only as good as the data and programming it uses. Principles, values, and ethics are inherent in algorithms and data collection. Data are a set of numbers or calculations. Analytics require critical thinking skills to determine the conclusions behind the data that guides decision making.

Metrics need to be definitely related to issues of real significance. Measure test scores? Measure graduation rates? Measure attitude? Commitment? Family structure? Some organizations collect what are called vanity metrics; for example, website visitors per month, media impressions, or number of "friends" that have little or no impact as a clear and accurate measure of performance.

Algorithms are powerful and generally unknown to artificial intelligence users, but they affect many aspects of people's lives that have powerful impacts and outcomes. According to a PEW study, many people do not real-ize the effect they have in recommended sites that are selected for them. Concerning Facebook, 74 percent of the users did not realize the site main-tained a list of user's interests and traits. Fifty-one percent indicated they were not comfortable with Facebook compiling this information.[6]

With algorithms, there's an issue of responsibility. They must not be open to manipulation. Some individuals may want to find flaws in the algorithm for their own purposes. When the system fails, who is responsible—the program-mers, the executive decision makers, the bureaucrats?

According to Bostrom and Yudkowsky, "Responsibility, transparency, auditability, incorruptibility, predictability, and a tendency to not make innocent victims scream with helpless frustration: all criteria that apply to humans performing social functions; all criteria that must be considered in an algorithm intended to replace human judgment of social functions; all criteria that may not appear in a journal of machine learning considering how an algorithm scales up to more computers. This list of criteria is by no means exhaustive, but it serves as a small sample of what an increasingly computer-ized society should be thinking about."[7]

Moral Status

While artificial intelligence can review great masses of data for use in decision making, there is one actual piece missing. Data is one thing, but ethics in its use is another. Situational conditions may, in fact, require a different direction than algorithms or machine learning may conclude. Efficiency or conventional conclusions should not subvert research principles, creativity, and values.

Many individuals confront a situation where the cognitive data indicated a rational reaction to impending circumstances. However, other nonmetrical and value-based circumstances demanded a different direction than what the artificial intelligence specified. Emotions and instinct, however, provide information and clarity on what really matters in life.

The concern may be based on ethics and values or emotional understanding. Acting ethically and morally might negate decisions on the basis of pure numerical rationality or on any actions at all. Social situations can move beyond a strict metrical instrumental rationality, based on the best means necessary to achieve a specific end. The assumption is that if there is reason to take an action, then any one of the possible plans to get to that end efficiently and in a cost-effective and efficient manner is rational based on data.

The question of ethics and values raises issues of "why" things are done and "how" they are completed: are they acceptable from a moral and ethical standpoint. Moral reasoning concerns what can be done versus what ought to be done. Living up to morals and ethics presents questions about solutions derived through instrumental rationality.

On a major historical level, on August 6, 1945, the United States dropped the first atomic bomb on Japan with the second one to follow. From a moral perspective, was this the right decision because of the obvious deaths of civilians—women, men, and children—who were noncombatants?

President Truman stated that there were three options: obtaining Russian involvement in the Pacific war, continuing the campaign through conventional bombing and naval blockades, or modifying President Franklin Roosevelt's commitment to unconditional surrender. The assertion was that these proposals would extend the war and cost thousands of American lives and others.

To this day, the morality of this decision is raised and discussed. Certainly, there are always ethical questions about warfare, which in itself often involves violating ethical and moral standards in order to protect the lives of others. The destruction of cities and their populations was already taking place. The atomic bombing required only one plane and one bomb.

The question raised was: was the atomic bomb necessary to end the war and save the lives of others in greater number? Or were there other measures or strategies available to limit the killing of civilians and children? Does it matter who dies: civilians or military personnel trained for warfare? Or is warfare value free: all deaths are of equal stature?

Historical decisions raise issues of morality. In everyone's life there are matters of instrumental rationality versus ethics and morality of decisions and outcomes. They often raise corollary questions of character, integrity, and fortitude.

Concerning machine morality, science fiction writer Isaac Asimov defined in his novels the three rules for robots that are cited today in articles on contemporary technology. "1. A robot may not injure a human being, or, through inaction, allow a human being to come to harm. 2. A robot must obey the orders given to it by human beings except where such orders would conflict with the First Law. 3. A robot must protect its own existence, as long as such protection does not conflict with the First or Second Law."[8]

As artificial intelligence progresses, issues of moral consequences are raised, some related to difficult possibilities if thinking machines become more prominent.

Privacy and Surveillance

Privacy is one of the major values of the United States. Today, a great deal of information is collected as sites maintain data about the location, personal preferences, reading, and Internet site selection of individuals. Americans are concerned about maintaining their privacy, because the prevalence of technology jeopardizes issues of exposure and publicity, as well as government or other surveillance.

What people explore on the Internet is a part of today's lifestyle. Databases and Internet sites maintain information and often propose to users other purchases or decisions they may like depending on their past history. Purchasing a book on Amazon on a certain subject causes other books to be suggested to the individual in the following days. In the past, where one went, researched, purchased, or emailed was only one's business, not Google's, Facebook's, Twitter's, or society generally. It raises issues of what one shares on technology-driven sites.

Government surveillance is always been anathema in American democracy. Surveillance is a prime foundation of totalitarian systems of control and discipline. While artificial intelligence can provide information, it can also control what individuals see or read. The site recommends content and books determined by algorithms and past interests. Search engines may not be totally open to providing content or sites determined by a person's interests or past behavior. In this process, other perspectives or viewpoints may not be presented. And, in some cases, some books, authors, or points of view can be promoted, censored, or ignored.

Today cameras are prevalent. Recognition systems, plus cell phones, can identify where individuals are or have been. Cell phones have a great deal of information about an individual's location, purchases, who they text or call, and other preferences. Smart phones and other technology are a far cry from the past because they can be addictive and used for propaganda.

The American Civil Liberties Union has been concerned for years about the possibility of governments using technology for the surveillance of civilians and propaganda. Some governments like China, for example, use cameras to determine where citizens are or have been. Repercussions or other fallout can occur. Should the government use facial recognition in urban and other areas as one of its tools under the guise of safety from crime and other threats?

Some universities are actually tracking students to ensure they attend class. For example, "When Syracuse University freshmen walk into . . . Introduction to Information Technologies class, seven small Bluetooth beacons hidden around the Grant Auditorium lecture hall connect with an app on their Smartphones and boost their attendance points."[9]

Artificial intelligence is difficult to regulate. Determining the values written into the algorithmic system is beyond a citizen's purview. "Lifting the lid" on technology and observing the standards and values on which it works is problematic for the common citizen to assess. Auditing the systems is extremely difficult. Should citizens simply have to believe and assume companies and the government are working ethically and correctly?

Obviously, there are benefits to AI and its ability for data analysis and providing services. But the system can be "gamed." The *Wall Street Journal* investigated the impact of interest groups on shaping what users see on Google. According to the study, Google executives consistently stated in congressional hearings that algorithms are objective and autonomous.

The article stated that Google made "changes to its search results that favor big businesses over smaller ones," the supposition being that the customers were more likely to get what they wanted from larger outlets than smaller ones. In addition,

Far from being autonomous computer programs oblivious to outside pressure, Google's algorithms are subject to regular tinkering from executives and engineers who are trying to deliver relevant search results, while also pleasing a wide variety of powerful interests and driving its parent company's more than $30 billion in annual profit. Google is now the most highly trafficked website in the world, surpassing 90 percent of the market share for all search engines.[10]

A major concern with the Internet and online research is that the algorithms on Amazon, Google, and other sites are neutral and simply scour the Internet objectively to get results. Companies modify algorithms and these modifications, slight as they may be and how they are interpreted, produce differences in results.

In a democracy, ethics matter. Free speech and access to information and opinion are absolute essentials. The power of technology and artificial intelligence can promote or stymie the freedom of speech. Free speech is not always going to be pleasant or accepted. In all totalitarian regimes control over information and thinking is a primary goal. People have been harassed and abused as a result of comments or opinions.

Burning books or limiting their circulation or firing individuals for their opinions or politics are contrary to a free society and not accepted.

Clueless Artificial Intelligence

Artificial intelligence captures people's imaginations. The general opinion is that it can do almost everything a person can do. But that is not the case!

A major issue in society and for true leadership is to determine "cause and effect." Leaders and governments must not only understand situations, but must be able to determine what caused or created them. "Understanding cause and effect is a big aspect of what we called common sense, and it's an area in which AI systems today are 'clueless,'"[11] according to Elias Bareinboim, the director of the Causal Artificial Intelligence Lab at Columbia University.

Causal reasoning is beyond artificial intelligence currently. It lacks common sense and cannot, in a deep way, infer what will result in a given action and situation. For example, what policy changes would improve public education? What if schools in . . .? That kind of reasoning is beyond today's artificial intelligence capability.

Judea Pearl, computer scientists at UCLA, asserted that artificial intelligence could not be truly intelligent until it understands cause and effect that enables the introspection at the core of cognition. Introspection and intuition, "what if queries," "are the building blocks of science, of moral attitudes, of free will, of consciousness."[12]

Within a new concept or renovation, there are positive and negative issues. Technology is a powerful tool. The question is: can it be used and applied to positive purposes and values. How are principles and ethical values assured by the time when machines can think? Artificial intelligence has deep potential and ability, but like other powerful innovations, it needs to be controlled, not be the controller.

NOTES

1. Gordon McCalle, "The Fragmentation of Culture, Learning, Teaching and Technology: Implications for the Artificial Intelligence in Educational Research

Agenda in 2010," *International Journal of Artificial Intelligence in Education* 11 (2000): 177–96.

2. Tim Fontaine, Brian McCarthy, and Tamin Saleh, "Building the AI-Powered Organization," *Harvard Business Review*, July–August 2019.

3. Mark Coeckelberg, *AI Ethics* (Cambridge, MA: The MIT Press, 2020), 128–29.

4. Stanford Medicine, Scope, "Can Artificial Intelligence Help Doctors with the Human Side of Medicine," https://scopeblog.stanford.edu/2018/12/12/can-artificial-intelligence-help-doctors-with-the-human-side-of-medicine/.

5. Marco Iansiti and Karim R. Lakhani, *Competing in the Age of AI* (Over Review Press, 2020), 182–84.

6. PEW, "7 Things We've Learned about Computer Algorithms," https://www.pewresearch.org/fact-tank/2019/02/13/7-things-weve-learned-about-computer-algorithms/.

7. Bostrom and Yudkowsky, op.cit. 2.

8. Melanie Mitchell, *Artificial Intelligence: A Guide for Thinking Humans* (New York: Farrar, Straus, and Giroux, 2019), Kindle edition, 126.

9. Drew Farwell, "Colleges Are Turning Students Phones into Surveillance Machines, Tracking the Locations of Hundreds of Thousands," *Washington Post*, December 24, 2019, https://www.washingtonpost.com/technology/2019/12/24/colleges-are-turning-students-phones-into-surveillance-machines-tracking-locations-hundreds-thousands/.

10. Ibid.

11. Brian Bergstein. "What AI Still Can't Do," *Technology Review*, February 19, 2020, https://www.technologyreview.com/2020/02/19/868178/what-ai-still-cant-do/.

12. Ibid.

Chapter 9

Implications

Education

Our education system has succeeded so far in teaching generations to do different routine tasks. So when tractors displaced farming labor, we taught the next generation to work in factories. But what we've never really been good at is teaching a huge number of people to do non-routine creative work.

—Andrew Ng, Computer Scientist

Transformation and change raise questions about education, some without clear answers. Does the purpose and aims of education enhance or limit transformation? Does creativity bring about necessary shifts in education to address the transformations that are occurring? What is the relationship between scientific transformation and education? Does education create the seeds that blossom into greater understanding and the development of innovation? What is the role of education to prepare students to understand what is emerging and changing?

Changes in cultural and economic conditions influence the focus of education and reform. During the transformation from agriculture to an industrial society, education focused on basic skills—reading, writing, and arithmetic—all necessary for being trained in machine operation and following managerial procedures and policies. Reliability, efficiency, and precision were required at work, along with consistency in carrying out responsibilities.

A complex society and economy necessitates moving beyond simple reading and math skills to intellectual and technical abilities, creativity, and very importantly philosophical understanding, the foundation of which is a strong education. Trust in political, economic, and social agencies and institutions is developed through understanding the principles and foundational values of the United States.

Citizens today require a strong ability to analyze and assess ideas and proposals. Adherence to basic and vital principles and values in a democracy and understanding moral standards is necessary. In addition, imagination and creativity are indispensable today.

Innovation is at the forefront of a growing economy and the incorporation of technology in all facets of life. Today, the emphasis on a "knowledge society," goes beyond simple academic skills and the mastery of facts. Complex, creative, and analytical thinking are required.

Transformation raises many questions of ethics and values. All societies and organizations have principles governing human behavior and interactions. Principles are unwavering and are at the core of society and culture determining the evaluation and consequences of behavior and actions. They establish the moral and ethical nature of society and culture.

Values create the standards for assessing ideas or issues. With the explosion of websites and information, understanding what is true, fabricated, distorted, or biased is essential. With the volume of commentary and expression, the question "What is truth?" is a basic staple of citizenship and professionalism.

In today's society, education of the few is a policy in failure. Being schooled is one thing, being educated is another. Education nurtures ability and talent, not simply obedience to specified ways. All citizens require a quality education, particularly in a time of transformation and when machines can think.

EDUCATION VS. SCHOOLING

Being well-schooled does not necessarily mean well educated. Years in school do not necessarily translate into being educated. A major concern today is what the core of education is in this day and age of technological and social change.

Instruction is very important. Simple recall, however, does not evolve into a comprehensive education. The current emphasis on test scores to determine school success narrows the definition of education. The assumption is: if children do well on standardized tests, then they are well educated. But that assumption is wrong.

Recall and regurgitation are not thinking. There are many examples of individuals with high test scores who made vacuous decisions that oppressed people, violated humanity, and destroyed civility and purpose. History books illustrate their impact on the world as well as American society.

Too often children perceive learning as a competitive exercise—test scores, grades, and honor rolls. Young children get the impression that they are not smart without realizing what intelligence and learning actually are. Being educated is not a competitive endeavor because learning and scholarship is a process of growing intellectually and requires time and commitment. It is not a contest of winning and acclaim.

Many students do not always recognize that a commitment to principles and hard work can overcome perceived limits and shortcomings. Human worth cannot be quantified by a set of numbers, discounting the intangibles of "heart," perseverance, and resolve. Commitment and hard work can overcome one's past and failures in childhood and adulthood.

Being well educated involves cognitive skills and understanding, ethics and values, independent thinking and analysis, philosophy, and creative cultural experiences. Synthesizing, understanding, analyzing, and evaluating ideas are cognitive thought processes necessary for making appropriate and wise decisions based on principle and values. All citizens need these abilities to meet their responsibilities.

In the book *The Fog of Reform*, Goens states, "The great philosophical questions of life—truth, beauty, justice, liberty, equality, and goodness—cannot be assessed through a computer scored test. Searching for answers to these issues is at the very core of our society and the essence of becoming well-educated."[1] These philosophical issues are ever present in most important personal, social, or political questions and decisions. Today, with the capability of artificial intelligence and other technology, these questions are even more relevant and highly important.

The six philosophical questions are pertinent in any period of life and history. While philosophical in tone, they are at the core of an educated society and a consequential individual life. All people, including children, deal with them in life, personally, professionally, and civilly. Knowledge comes and goes as research in cognitive understanding increases. However, life is complete with personal and social relationships. At the core are philosophical principles and ideas. They are essential for an honorable and meaningful life. A major responsibility in life is to make principled decisions. Their adherence to values and ethics is essential for family and governance.

Students must understand that they have an impact on not only their individual life but also the world around them. Education is more than training and conforming to assembly-line mentality. Artificial intelligence will take care of that and more. People require a strong academic and principle-centered program so they can contribute personally, socially, and ethically over their entire lifespan in ways that are beyond the capability of algorithmically directed artificial intelligence.

A knowledge-driven economy and the rise of ubiquitous data and information require that "Education will become the center of the knowledge society, and the school its key institution. What knowledge must everybody have? What is 'quality' in learning and teaching? These will of necessity become central concerns of the knowledge society, and central political issues. In fact, the acquisition and distribution of formal knowledge may come to occupy the place in the politics of the knowledge society which the acquisition and distribution of property and income have occupied in our politics over the two or three centuries that we have come to call the Age of Capitalism."[2]

Technology shapes American life for everyone. Some of the changes are obvious and others less so. Convenience, speed, and comfort are fairly clear. But Neil Postman in his book *Technopoly* indicated that the emphasis on quantitative approaches and technology is a step in constructing a mathematical concept of reality. He stated, "To say that someone should be doing better work because he has an IQ of 134, or that someone is a 7.2 on the sensitivity scale, or that this man's essay and the rise of capitalism is an A- and that man's is a C+ would have sounded like gibberish to Galileo or Shakespeare or Thomas Jefferson. We see the world differently than they did because our minds have been conditioned by the technology of numbers.

Our understanding of what is real is different. Which is another way of saying that embedded in every tool is an ideological bias, a predisposition to construct the world as one thing rather than another, to value one thing over another, to amplify one sense or skill or attitude more loudly than another.[3]

In essence, individuals have to learn how to learn, which is indispensable in all transformational times. Continued education is necessary for professional or economic life, particularly since the impact of a revolutionary innovation like artificial intelligence brings about new ideas and capabilities for institutions and mankind.

AI AND HUMANS

Artificial intelligence is becoming an integral aspect of life. In fact, it is probably more prevalent than most people realize: online in their search engines, business purchases, data management, banking, speech recognition, and other aspects of life from the routine to complex professional and governmental services.

While this expansion increases abilities and efficiencies, it also poses concerns, some quite serious personally, socially, and politically. The research conducted by the PEW Research Center titled "Artificial Intelligence and the Future of Humans" canvassed 797 technology leaders, innovators, developers, business and policy leaders, researchers, and activists about whether people will be "better off than they are today" as artificial intelligence continues to expand.

"The experts predicted networked artificial intelligence will amplify human effectiveness but also threaten human autonomy, agency and capabilities. They spoke of the wide-ranging possibilities; that computers might match or even exceed human intelligence and capabilities on tasks such as complex decision-making, reasoning and learning, sophisticated analytics and pattern recognition, visual acuity, speech recognition and language translation. They said 'smart' systems in communities, in vehicles, in buildings and utilities, on farms and in business processes will save time, money and lives and offer opportunities for individuals to enjoy a more-customized future."[4]

No innovation or transformational move is without a dark side. How they are implemented is dependent on insight, discernment, attitudes, philosophical principles, and ethics. In this research, technology experts identified concerns:

- Control: individuals are experiencing a loss of control over their lives because they defer to "codes" driving algorithms (blackbox tools), thus they sacrifice independence, privacy, and the power over choice. People have no direct control over these automated systems, which can have algorithmic biases.
- Data Abuse: Data use and surveillance is designed for profit or for exercising power. Values and ethics are not inked into digital systems that make decisions for people. What is most efficient may not be the most ethical or compassionate. Some people are willing to give up privacy for the ease that artificial intelligence provides.
- Job Loss: As discussed earlier, the automation of jobs widens the economic gap and creates some social upheaval. New jobs will be created but not guaranteed to be in the same number and will require different knowledge, abilities, and skills.
- Dependence: Some experts predict because of technological capability that individuals' cognitive, social, and survival skills will diminish. Dependence, they believe, on machine-driven networks erodes people's ability to think for themselves, interact with others, and make decisive actions independent of automated systems. Many people do not understand that links written in text or algorithms can also have a bias.
- Mayhem: some predict that autonomous weapons, cybercrime, and "weaponized information" will erode sociopolitical structures, the control of weapons of warfare, and "weaponize" information that can destabilize society. These concerns not only apply to international issues, they also impact American society and culture as well.

Algorithms determine if biases are at play in website data and analysis. Bias destroys trust, which is a major matter, particularly for governance and news and information sites. Approximately 41 percent trust the news and other websites in reporting the news objectively and accurately. Technology provides data and information, but is it accurate or unbiased? Numbers can lie if they are not collected and analyzed properly. Data must be unbiased and accurate in its collection, as well as analysis.

These possibilities obviously erode values and ethics, in part because individuals do not thoroughly understand the technology or the concerns at stake. Some issues are invisible, for example, algorithmic focus is out of sight, which too often means out of mind. Convenience and speed cause people to overlook values and possible consequences. Citizens cannot "get off the hook" because their ignorance curtailed ethics and fed the subterranean power of unknown principles and of technological programming. Experts suggest developing policies to assure that artificial intelligence will be directed at the "common good" and meets social and ethical responsibilities.

HUMAN INTELLIGENCE

People must be a priority: their capabilities and capacities must be expanded to heighten the collaboration of humans, artificial intelligence, and other sources. Human relevance must not be compromised in facing artificial and programmed intelligence.

In the final analysis, 63 percent of the thought leaders in the PEW study were hopeful that individuals would be better off in 2030. On the other side of the ledger, over a third, 37 percent, stated that people would not be better off. A major issue is ensuring that technology is in harmony with the nation's values.

Human beings have unique qualities that are difficult to replicate: they are complex, original, and one of a kind. They come with physical differences and mental capacities. They do not paint by the numbers, always following routine patterns and thinking. Some notice things that others cannot see or discern. There is a complicated individualism that is unique to each person's ability to perceive, think, and feel about life.

Unique human characteristics revolve around creativity and flexibility. Creativity is evident in everyone's life to some degree, and obviously, individuals apply imagination, ingenuity, and inventiveness in their lives. No two humans are the same: physically they operate the same, but not intellectually—humanly. Originality and expressiveness are unique to each individual as is their artistry and perspective. Creative talent and vision are attributes that do not emanate through algorithmic thinking. Emotional sensitivity is not artificial.

In life there are times when actions based on rational analysis are not appropriate or correct. Emotions and feelings, at times, detect instinctive options or solutions that would not be considered in a linear flowchart or diagram. They may not be clearly evident or seen but are "felt" or "heartfelt" inside. Instinct and intuition provide a subconscious feeling concerning decisions and what direction should be taken—seeing the world through intuition and several lenses is a positive approach.

Obviously, people have cognitive as well as emotional challenges requiring the ability to make decisions, understand their emotional impacts, and have the unique ability to apply imagination and creativity to circumstances. Sometimes what seems the most logical response or the one most accepted by others is not the correct course. The heart, at times, makes more sense than the brain.

EDUCATION, THINKING, AND ETHICS

Technology is supposed to help with decision making and problem solving. To do so, individuals require their own solid, independent thinking ability to assess all aspects of an important question in order to make critical decisions.

Thinking is not simply recalling facts and figures. It is much more. There are four important critical thinking skills—some more complex than others.

The basic skill—convergent analytical thinking—is what most individuals perceive thinking to be: logically coming up with the best answer to the matter at hand. Memory, logic, and available resources assist in solving issues that do not require creative or lateral thinking.

A second category, divergent thinking, is the opposite of convergent thought in that it involves coming up with solutions or pathways when no single explanation exists. To do so requires the ability to develop several solutions to a matter without clear answers. Being able to break down possibilities into pros and cons and consider each one is a part of the process.

Critical thinking is a goal requiring analysis and judgment. Deductive conclusions are formulated on available facts. Induction applies critical thinking skills to draw conclusions based on a generalization because all the facts are not available.

Creative thinking is the fourth level, involving forming perspective and making decisions in an unconditional or unusual manner. A creative thinker finds holes in the thinking of others and proposes a different insight and point of view, along with new or unique ways to address the issue or problem.

Different facets of life or questions require analysis, problem solving, and creativity. Open-mindedness and flexibility are essential when examining problems and dilemmas. Posing questions along with intellectual flexibility is often needed in contending with dilemmas and new or contrasting points of view.

As in the past, critical thinking is necessary: analyzing ideas and assessing the upsides and downsides of them. Things are not always logical and what is apparent may not always be true. Systems thinking is also necessary to analyze issues across areas in an interdisciplinary vein: seeing the interrelatedness of ideas, issues, and proposals.

Systems analysis involves seeing a broad perspective including the overall structure, pattern, interconnections, and operational cycles. It is a broad view that enables deeper analysis of systems to make reliable inferences. Computers are good at convergent thinking: finding a single correct answer to a problem or task. Education is focused on convergent thinking, which was very important in an industrialized society. Many standardized and teacher-made tests are based on this concept.

Divergent thinking, however, involves generating multiple responses in the application of curiosity and creativity to recommendations and decisions. Artificial intelligence is efficient at convergent tasks. But today, a major challenge is creativity. Certainly understanding math, science, social studies, and English is important as basic tools along with the skills behind them.

A critical component of education in a technological society is ethics. Artificial intelligence raises many ethical questions and issues:

- How do artificial intelligence machines and processes align with basic values?
- Can artificial intelligence deal with issues when two ethical principles collide?
- If artificial intelligence causes harm, who is morally culpable?
- How is a quality assured?
- In analysis?
- In services like health care?
- In reorganization of the workplace?

There are ramifications of artificial intelligence and politics, economics, law, philosophy, culture, ethics, and education.

Technological literacy involves mathematics, coding, and basic operation of artificial intelligence and is necessary so individuals understand the strengths and limitations of technology. Comprehending the logic behind programming is essential. Many people believe that if information or decisions come from a computer that they must be correct—that it is unbiased. This perspective requires education in another area—data literacy.

Data literacy provides the background to understanding how systems work and how to make sense of data. Understanding the parameters of data in the social, scientific, economic, and political context is necessary. Because it comes from data, does that mean it is accurate based on research and proper data selection and analysis? Sample size and nature, methods of analysis, and the questions of how they are presented are just a few of the concerns for technological analysis. The web is filled with data—how do you know it is correct?

EDUCATION AND HISTORY

History also plays a role, influenced by the various preceding economic and social transformations that transpired. Education is perceived as a foundation for life, not simply for employment. In dark economic times—recession and depression—education is seen as the doorway to good jobs, flexibility, and the good life with options and choices.

As times evolve, the nature and focus of education becomes a topic of controversy. This evolution led to accountability based on tests and metrics. Education, however, is necessary for thinking acuity and expertise. One does not have to be a program writer for computers but simply be able to ask the pertinent questions about data collection and its integrity to research.

Understanding philosophy and principles of relationships and governance are absolutely essential. In addition, being able to think and analyze in a number of different ways is necessary in all aspects of one's life. Being able to recognize the assumptions behind arguments and policies is necessary to evaluate the impact on people and principles.

A prime historical example is the rise of Nazi Germany. Daniel Lattier wrote: "This all occurred in what was, or at least seemed by the late 19th century to be, Europe's most culture, certainly it's best-educated country. Germany had the world's finest elementary school system, the highest literacy rate and the best universities; by 1913 more books were published annually in Germany than in any country in the world."[5]

Some Nazi leaders were well-schooled: Joseph Goebbels had a doctorate in philology (a branch of knowledge dealing with the structure, historical development, and relationships of a language or languages). Albert Speer was an architect, and some well-educated German professionals advocated for the Nazi's positions.

Exemplary test scores do not produce ethical conduct, which was apparent in Nazi Germany and other historical totalitarian regimes. While leaders had the diplomas, they lacked an ethical framework to govern their life and decisions. While well-schooled, they made brutal and immoral decisions that injured and murdered thousands of people and were totally destructive to a civil society. History demonstrates the importance of education, not just schooling and getting a degree—values and morals and complex thinking are practical aspects of learning and education.

There are many examples of administrations packed with the "best and brightest" individuals with Ivy League law degrees and doctorates with demonstrated knowledge of facts, concepts, and theories. The Nixon administration had smart people, some of who made foolish decisions, even at times unethical and illegal ones. The question is: were they well educated or well-schooled?

Several false assumptions are evident in children's education. A primary question is: Are teachers solely responsible for students' performance in school? Family life, structure, and parental influence have extremely potent effects on children's attitude, discipline, and personal responsibility and conduct.

Too often, people or the media blame schools or teachers when the home context and environment are major forces for poor educational results. A student's mind, thinking, and perception are initially established in the family. Certainly, a quality education can raise questions about how children examine relationships, problems, and ethics. Lack of standards of conduct and structure debilitate a child's education. Children need to understand norms and values and be accountable for their own conduct by parents and schools.

Good parenting gives students a leg up because children need consistent standards to which they are held. Both parents must be involved and on the same page because consistent values and principles between parents are necessary. Some parents do not realize that setting clear standards for children is a clear expression of their love for them. Negotiating with children about their behavior is damaging to developing their responsibility for their thinking and behavior.

A second major fallacy is that education is strictly about preparation for making a living. Life involves more and is larger than earning a paycheck. Finding passion and meaning is important because they nurture happiness and satisfaction. Sometimes that is achieved through employment, but it is also the result of family, interests, talent, and principles. Continued learning and insight are indispensable for finding meaning: doing more than simply meeting personal economic or egotistical needs. Learning occurs throughout life—not just in school. Experience with failures and success, losses and gains, planned or unforeseen, provides a basis for greater understanding and possibly wisdom.

EDUCATION: HOW?

Through modeling and presenting a culture and climate of individual respect and dignity, individuals can grow. As moral agents, teachers need to be sure that the values of justice, fairness, and respect are accorded all children.

Schools have another primary purpose of responsibility that will serve students throughout their lives, as well as with others. Philosopher Mortimer

Adler stated that students and people "need the goods of the mind, such intellectual virtues as knowledge, understanding, a modicum of wisdom, both practical and speculative, together with such goods of the mind's activity as the liberal arts—the skills of inquiry and of learning, the habits of critical judgment and creative production."

Science, technology, engineering, and mathematics (STEM) are important, but they are not sufficient. Without a deep ethical understanding, knowledge can be manipulated and applied improperly and immorally. Knowing the language and skills of STEM is a part of the equation, but individuals' lives personally, socially, and creatively require much more.

Knowledge—its acquisition, development, and understanding, along with conceptual ideas and values—are essential. Society needs artists and philosophers as much as scientists and engineers. This is basic for all people and fundamental in order to meet life's requirements and challenges.

According to Adler's proposal for education, the Paideia Proposal (from the Greek word *paidos* concerning the upbringing of a child), the acquisition of knowledge can be done through a variety of means in order to learn subject matter and language, literature, fine arts, mathematics, science, history, geography, and social studies.

A major component is a development of intellectual skills of learning through practice, coaching, and exercises. The skill areas include reading, writing, listening, speaking, calculating, problem solving, observing, measuring, estimating, and exercising critical judgment.

A final valuable area of education concerns a deeper understanding of ideas and values, which can be done through Socratic questioning and active participation in discussions, books, philosophy, works of art, drama, visual arts, and ideas and values. Socratic questioning is a form of argumentative dialogue where two people ask and answer questions to draw out ideas and promote critical thinking. To engage in discourse individuals must be able to raise questions and answers in order to understand the other individual's responses and beliefs. Logic is important, as is a positive and respectful relationship.

Howard Gardner indicated that education involves "Mastering disciplines, learning to communicate effectively, engaging civilly in discussion and argument—these have and should remain at the forefront of all education. The ancients talked about the importance of understanding what is true (and what is not); what is beautiful (and what is not worth lingering over); and what is good (in terms of being a worthy person, worker, and citizen). These educational goals should be perennial."[6] Today, in the United States, knowing truth from bluster or propaganda is necessary for all citizens in all phases and areas of life.

A quality education focuses on acquiring knowledge, developing intellectual skills, and understanding ideas and values. All children would be exposed to the same content knowledge to include language, literature, fine arts, mathematics, natural science, history, geography, and social studies. Reading, didactic presentations, and student responses are the means to gain knowledge.

Mastering skills and concepts in reading, writing, speaking, researching, mathematics, reasoning, problem solving, questioning, analyzing, synthesizing, and thinking provides a necessary foundation for children to become well-educated. Questioning is an important method. Questions range from simple knowledge and recall to the more complex ones of analysis, synthesis, and evaluation. Higher-order questions require a depth of thinking to respond to them.

These essential skills enable children to learn the significant concepts that are the foundations for communication, mathematics, science, social science, and the arts. Concepts and ideas in these academic areas, however, are not discrete because they are vital in applying critical judgment. Seeing connections between and across content, concepts, and theories and being able to think critically and imaginatively about them are basic to citizenship and civil discussion.

Schools should fan the creative sparks in children because society needs innovation and imaginative citizens. Historically, the standing of the United States, the American Dream, as well as the economy and society rests on innovation, ingenuity, and the creativity of individuals. To flourish as a culture, children's innate imaginative heart must be nurtured and developed. The arts and other programs that encourage imaginative thinking have for too long been stepchildren in schools. The arts are powerful venues for critical judgments and perspective across all areas of life.

Socratic dialogue is an old but effective method of challenging students' thought processes and reasoning. Students must answer questions followed by subsequent questions that require them to analyze and assess their logic, reasoning, and understanding. These are basic skills of civility and citizenship. Socratic dialogue can also be used in discussions with public officials, policymakers, and others.

Socratic questioning and active participation leads to comprehension and understanding of ideas and values. Discussing books, political ideas (freedom and equality), as well as formal presentations spurs understanding. These activities require students to confront ideas, assess them, and present them in a formal manner. Students of all ages can learn through discussion and seminars that are age appropriate.

Education moves deeper than skills to a greater understanding of concepts, values, principles, and the relationship of content and context, ideas, civility, thinking, ethics, the arts, and intelligence. Being well-educated ultimately should develop highly capable thinkers and understanding of principles and their accurate definition and application.

Wisdom is seldom mentioned when discussing education. It is not the regurgitation of facts or simple memory. It is not a competitive goal measured via a metrically driven test. There is a distinction between being smart and wise. Wisdom is not simply the province of the more elderly in society. Can technology be wise or is it only smart?

Wisdom grows out of the heart and the intellect, encompassed within insight, judgment, discernment, and understanding. As Socrates stated, "the only true wisdom is in knowing you know nothing."

Wisdom requires the intelligent application of knowledge coupled with the quality of deep insight into what is ethical and virtuous. Wisdom concerns values and the use of knowledge and good judgment. Character is based on it. Everyone wants children to move beyond facts and figures and become "good" people who act on the basis of their knowledge, principles, and hearts, which when melded with values are powerful influences on their character and life's outcomes.

NOTES

1. George A. Goens, *The Fog of Reform* (Lanham, MD: Rowman and Littlefield, 2016), 58.

2. Peter Drucker, "Age of Social Transformation," *Atlantic*, December 1995, https://www.theatlantic.com/past/docs/issues/95dec/chilearn/drucker.htm.

3. Neil Postman, *Technopoly* (New York: Vintage Keflex, 1993), 13.

4. PEW, "Artificial Intelligence and the Future of Humans," https://www.pewresearch.org/internet/2018/12/10/artificial-intelligence-and-the-future-of-humans/.

5. Daniel Lattier, "Nazi Germany Was Highly Educated," https://www.intellectualtakeout.org/blog/nazi-germany-was-highly-educated/.

Chapter 10

Human Beings

It seems to me that one of the most distinctive features of human intelligence is the capacity to imagine, to project out of our immediate circumstances and to bring to mind things that are present here and now.

—Ken Robinson

It's beyond the limits of human intelligence to understand how human intelligence works.

—Noam Chomsky

One thing is clearly evident in everyone's life from birth to death. Living means changing. Though change and its nature are evident, outcomes are not fully known. Sometimes only in retrospect do individuals fully comprehend what happened and its consequences. History is not always immediately observable. Tangible and intangible forces influence each other and move at a tempo not easily detected. Transformation brings much more—specifically, unknowns.

Things emerge and evolve—some at different paces and depth. Transformation is a deep shift in structure and systems and opens the door to major economic, social, and cultural conversions. An old mindset about how life will play out is challenged. How things unfold is not clear: sometimes minor incidents or circumstances generate huge repercussions. Lack of clarity raises confusion and fear, and planning becomes difficult when threads and dynamics are unknown. What is obvious is not always of great consequence.

What does one do and think in unsettled times? "Old days" are receding as the new ones present uncertain opportunities in meeting one's individual and family's needs. Confidence comes with certainty. Ambiguity, speculation, and uncertainty are very disturbing. However, there are no clear models for how and where transformation is going to impact various facets of life. Comprehending the nature and total consequences of transformation is beyond an individual's control because things evolve at their own pace.

Life seldom evolves the way people assume. In childhood, kids dream of becoming athletic stars or famous performers. Expectations based on dreams are important to have, but children learn, grow, and adapt to the evolution and interests in their lives and the unexpected ones that society and culture present.

People must reorient their point of view or direction to the fundamental changes taking place. Analyzing new prospects and expectations requires thought and understanding: thinking deeper and being analytical and proactive.

Achieving success and happiness requires the pursuit of purpose with passion.[1] Purpose concerns working toward a mission or ideal that is larger than oneself: to produce results that have a credible impact or goal. People are driven in their work to achieve the desired results, and by doing so create a legacy for children, family, and others. Even failing can be a positive example of principle and determined commitment—raising and addressing issues of principle and virtue requires nerve. Passion comes from the heart and is related directly to a calling because it is intrinsically motivating. It is something greater than simply finishing a task or job for compensation.

Transformational issues have the depth of change and intensity. What is at risk in these times is one's identity. In the past, individuals recognized who they were: interests, personality, work, and role in the family and community. Emotionally, they understood who they were and so did others. They comprehended how they got to where they are, and what it took to get there. Comfort stems from consistency and recognizing how things work.

Great cultural alterations have major implications. Tension arises because personal values can be out of harmony, and this disharmony raises conflict because what is emerging is not totally known or understood. If the individual's values are in accord with the transformation, commitment and satisfaction are greater.

How different generations perceive some of the social and cultural changes are examples of this tendency. Change is perceived through one's lens of values and norms, and if it is viewed as contrary to them, individuals will resist or negate them. Emotions and behavior are either exacerbated or calmed given their view of situations. People react more determinedly if the transformation conforms to or challenges their perceptions and values. Those who favor it will be strong advocates, and if they disagree, they will be very active resistors. A positive emotion toward the alterations may also induce impatience: can't wait for this to happen or to end.

The prospect of negative change triggers trepidation and a sense that things are collapsing. Some feel a sense of failure for not being more proactive in the past that would have addressed the issues they face today. Being shortsighted in retrospect is exasperating.

These times also bring confusion because explanations of what is occurring may be unclear, at odds with each other, or incomplete. Confusion also arises when one's heart and head conflict. Times exist where individuals believe in the values and future that is unfolding, but intellectually they resist because of the significance to them personally, socially, and economically. Change can daunt a sense of purpose.

Coming to grips with ambiguity and turmoil is not easy when a new path is evolving. If individuals define themselves by their job or external recognition, any compromise of them limits the support for new programs. Some have difficulty recognizing their feelings and why they have them. Not understanding the trajectory and the extent of change can be depressing and frustrating, causing individuals to shut themselves off from the external world. They shut down and stop communication with friends, colleagues, and family.

Redefining oneself may be necessary in these times. Looking internally helps to identify what one values and opens possible courses and approaches to be true to themselves. The intellect and heart work together to identify a purpose and a pathway. Wishing for what was is wishing for the impossible: the river of life moves on and requires adjustments.

According to Bob Tipton, there are nine stages in dealing with substantial change.[2] The status quo is safe and predictable. As things begin to change, however, people deny that it is taking place. They are shocked or simply amazed that events are occurring. Others simply thought it would not even take place. Because the status quo is familiar, individuals are inclined to resist change and the uncertainty it brings and get angry because the status quo and the comfort it generates is receding.

Anger is expected because of the unknowns—personally and professionally—that might evolve affecting other aspects of life. This can lead to bargaining or wishful thinking, which are normal when faced with serious change. In many of these situations, individuals look back and use the term "if only . . . If only, I . . . ," "if only Congress . . ." and a litany of others they face might have altered the transition.

Another stage is skepticism, in which people have choices. They can stay in place and live in despair and anger, continually looking back, flameout and give up on the change and seeking respite in a new organization. Or they can move forward with the change and grow in the new circumstances, basically, moving forward and eliminating the negativity.

From agreement comes advocacy, which is not easy to attain: it is a very major step. Many may agree with the transitions but not actively advocate for them. Advocates are positive agents of the transformation, moving far from a simple acceptance to looking ahead and advocating conversion.

Transformational change is never going to have 100 percent of the people and citizens advocating for it because it brings displacement and requires new skills and knowledge. People, at times, are displaced and have to move or change roles. At a certain point, they must come to grips with the fact that their old work is a thing of the past and accept the future. Individuals must question their assumptions and become freer to examine their beliefs and attitudes toward what is transpiring. Not an easy thing.

Self-management in transformational times is necessary to focus and achieve a level of calm that is constructive. Mindsets are important and can either energize people or cement them in place. Understanding reality and its positive and negative consequences and phases is necessary in order to make quality and appropriate decisions.

HUMAN AGENCY

Often people think of artificial intelligence as benign: simply there to make lives better and more efficient. But like every innovation, there are pluses and minuses. Some people only look at things or ideas from the "bright side": only the positives. Reality, however, is not that simple as good ideas can result in negative events or conditions and produce serious ethical questions or impacts for people.

Human agency, according to Albert Bandura of Stanford University, is using sensory and cerebral systems to "make their way successfully through a complex world full of challenges and hazards, people have to make sound judgments about the capabilities, anticipate the probable effects of different events and courses of action, size up sociostructural opportunities and constraints, and regulate their behavior accordingly."[3]

In essence, agency concerns individuals' control over their lives. In the PEW study[4] on "Artificial Intelligence and the Future of Humans," the experts involved cited concerns about AI and human agency. The five most often mentioned were:

- AI reduces individuals' control over their lives.
- Surveillance and data systems designed primarily for efficiency, profit, and control are inherently dangerous to individual and social privacy.
- Displacement of human jobs by AI will widen economic divides and possibly lead to social upheaval.
- Individuals' cognitive, social, and survival skills will be diminished as they become dependent on artificial intelligence.
- Citizens face increased vulnerabilities by cybercrime and cyber warfare and weaponized information.

Too often people have blind dependence on AI as it becomes more complex and powerful. Ownership of the AI systems by corporations or elites may have interests not always in accord with the general public, cultural, ethics, or national principles.

While artificial intelligence offers many benefits, it is not capable of things that are unique to humans. In actuality, those things are at the core of being human.

Artificial intelligence is totally impotent in any way to be empathetic toward people and their circumstances. Defining cognitive definitions—maybe. Demonstrating heartfelt empathy—not at all. Artificial intelligence is basically emotionless and cannot read people's feelings or intentions accurately.

Feelings and emotions are beyond the ability of AI to express: after all, they are programmed cognitively to respond in specific cognitive ways. Expressing feelings and unique forms of physical expression, touch, speech, humor, or satire are far beyond AI. Can technology express "heartfelt" emotion(s) when it operates solely by cognitive algorithms?

Analytics are inept at human emotion and social connection. Intangibles, intuition, emotion, and commitment are out of AI's capability. How would artificial intelligence respond to specific and varied emotional circumstances? Feelings are unique to situations and presence—being there emotionally is far beyond artificial intelligences capability.

Compassion and sense of belonging are not going to be expressed because emotion is seen and felt. It is communicated silently through energy and expression. Is it possible to write algorithms to fully understand and express emotional care or real emotional understanding? Human beings communicate through words, symbols, gestures, and facial expressions and distinctive expression and intentions—even silence. Individuals have energy around them through which they silently communicate attitudes and feelings.

Emotions are more than cognitive expressions. Human beings all have uniqueness that cannot be duplicated and their emotional needs may not be what is expected. People's lives are not totally the result of cognitive, linear thinking and behavior. Understanding how individuals are feeling is a unique human quality that comes by getting to know and understand individuals and their stories, values, and beliefs. Empathy requires that a person place themselves in someone else's shoes and actually feel as they do. Feelings, physical expressions, tone of voice, and touch are all aspects of emotional expression. Sometimes, silence is the best response.

Human understanding comes from experience, failure, success, anger, loss, and other emotions that cannot be easily written into algorithms. The depth of life experiences cannot be programmed because the impact is not the same for all people experiencing similar circumstances.

Artificial intelligence does not capture the true, complex nature of human thought and feeling because complex matters and nuances are not intelligible to it. Everyone gathers information through a variety of means: eyesight, listening, touching and feeling, past experiences, education, values, and others. Artificial intelligence follows an algorithm that cannot act on emotions and feelings. Anxious people may interpret events and communication differently than those who are at peace with circumstances. Artificial intelligence is just that—artificial. While it is helpful, there are concerns. People have innate qualities that all the algorithmic artificial intelligence will never have in a real human sense.

Values, personally and socially, are important. Algorithms can be and are written based on norms and values in terms of data and analysis. But there is a problem. Life is complex; some of the most difficult issues are the conflict between two or more positive values or principles or ignoring data and acting on emotional understanding.

Data does not really assess situations and circumstances thoroughly. Everyone at one time or another circumvented the rationality of numerical data and did the right thing to be successful. Situations that cannot be thoroughly understood through metrics may be settled through intuitive thought, experienced insight, and principled perspectives. Linear thinking based on metrical analysis does not define human motivation, feelings, or attitudes. Situations and "rightness" are more complicated than a universally applied algorithm, even if it learns.

A principle like always telling the truth can create problems. For example, if telling the truth will cost individuals their lives, should people be truthful? In totalitarian countries, telling the truth resulted in incarceration and death because of the corrupt values of the leadership and regime. In Germany, during Nazi rule, truth was deadly. The moral thing some circumstance requires is to lie in order to save a life.

Creativity is also the domain of human beings. AI cannot think outside the algorithm: out-of-the-box creativity is not in the equation because it basically does what it is directed to do, even though the more data collected can alter outcomes. Even confronting new situations, artificial intelligence relies on past algorithmic decisions and past analyses. Creative talent moves beyond the purpose of typical computer technology and is needed and essential.

Totally new ideas and directions, however, are the province of human beings. Nuance brings change, and technology does not have it. Creativity emanates from ideas and new perspectives. People apply synthesis from various areas and develop a whole new idea. Individuals take risks to develop something from new perspectives and experiences. Risks and uncertainties do not always stop people from making decisions.

Creativity involves the association of ideas, perception, analogical thinking, and reflection. Cognitive skills are necessary, but also emotion and motivation to come up with new and novel ideas and perspectives, which are surprising and invaluable. New perspectives come from creative energy and out-of-the-box (algorithmic) thinking.

Technology can combine ideas and help people gain perspective on the past generations of ideas. It can gather data about former approaches to persistent problems. It can help reduce human error in some areas of problematic behavior. But . . . it cannot be creative.

RELATIONSHIPS

Technology and social media reinforce or weaken human relationships. Being online and having faces on screens reduces the amount of time people have for real, in-person connections. Technological connections can be a very distracting force. People need to put their devices away and listen and talk in person with others without distraction. Listening is becoming a lost skill as individuals just text their attitudes and are unavailable for a real in-depth and revealing conversation.

In today's world people must be aware not only of events and relationships in their own lives but also in the larger picture. Mindfulness requires being aware and attentive to what is transpiring around them. In doing so, that understanding helps people manage the uncertainties that arise and begin to reflect and take positive responses.

Mindfulness requires "being focused on reality in the present moment in a state of nonjudgment, with acceptance and acknowledgment of what is."[5] Individuals must pay attention to what is unfolding as well as to their thoughts and internal emotions. It does not mean reacting to things in the usual way but discerning what really is happening and find the correct path. Mindfulness enhances the ability to maintain perspective, understand others' reactions, and improve the ability to interact with others.

A historian and computer scientist discussed the promise and perils of transformative technology. Yuval Noah Harari, an author of history and the future of the human species, and Fei-Fei Li, a pioneer in the field of artificial intelligence, were the major participants in a dialogue by the Stanford Center for Ethics and Society.[6]

Harari raised the issue that "human agency and individual freewill are being challenged like never before." He explained: "the ability to hack humans: to create an algorithm that understands me better than I understand myself, and can therefore manipulate me, enhance me, or replace me. And this is something that our philosophical baggage and all our belief in, you know, human agency and free will, and the customer is always right, and the voter knows best. It just falls apart once you have this kind of ability."

Harari also stated that more and more personal decisions are being outsourced to an algorithm because many believe that they are more capable than their own human ability. "We have the dystopia of surveillance capitalism, in which there is no like Big Brother dictator, but more and more of your decisions are being made by an algorithm. And it's not just decisions about what to eat or where to shop, but decisions like where to work and where to study, and whom to date and whom to marry and whom to vote for. It's the same logic. And I would be curious to hear if you think that there is anything in humans, which is by definition unhackable. We can't reach a point where the algorithm can make that decision better than me. So that's one line of dystopia, which is a bit more familiar in this part of the world. And then you have the full-fledged dystopia of a totalitarian regimes based on a total surveillance system. Something like the totalitarian regime that we have seen in the 20th century but augmented with biometric sensors and the ability to basically track each and every individual 24 hours a day."

Artificial intelligence brings strong capabilities but also serious and significant issues that need to be discussed. Certainly the application of artificial intelligence and its possibilities and assists need to be understood. The science and history behind it provides an understanding of innovation, change, and transformation. Artificial intelligence has highlighted some important policies and principles. Some are issues beyond employment and pertain to democracy.

A major concern is privacy. In a democratic society individuals have a right to maintain the privacy of their affairs. Only totalitarian regimes track citizen's movement, conversations, fiscal affairs, education, and other involvement without due process. Surveillance to artificial intelligence technology, cameras, voice recognition, and other communication methods is not appropriate unless approved through the legal process and means. Nor should citizens' privacy online, phones, or other means to be invaded by government, employers, or other agencies.

Artificial intelligence has also raised the major question—truth. Education is about thinking and analyzing content and circumstances to discern the truth. Critical thinking and analysis are essential for people in a democracy. Free speech does not ensure it is accurate or correct. People need to find reliable sources and apply critical assessment of content and sources in order to discern the truth from opinion.

Determining the principles for truth versus opinion is necessary to ensure being able to communicate responsibly and ethically to ensure reputation and standing remain positive. Being deceitful creates a loss of credibility.

The ability to listen clearly for the content and intent of messages and communication is necessary for citizenship as well as for any other aspect of a citizen's life. Citizens require critical and analytical thinking skills. Comprehending the content and intent of technology is as important as understanding the content and intent of communications, conversations, or documents. Skepticism is necessary.

Being skeptical is not a negative. Too often what is said politically, socially, or economically is not what is meant. Proposals and ideas are positives and negatives. All citizens in all roles need to be skeptical to understand the objectives and outcomes of proposals and policies. Skeptical thinking is geared to fully understanding the values and outcomes of ideas. Too often people are "sold a bill of goods" with consequences that are negative or harmful.

Ethics and appropriate use and application of data must be in concert with values. People must be educated on the ethics of citizenry and humanity, otherwise technology can lead people astray in its analyses and use.

Human beings have the power of the human spirit and it cannot be replicated. It is not standardized or manufactured. The human spirit comes from the mind, heart, and soul. Artificial intelligence will never replicate the individualism that is unique to each person. Falling in love. Creativity. Passion. Sentiment. Tenderness. All of them with their unique and indescribable emotion and connection are beyond intellectual programming of technology—artificial intelligence or not.

NOTES

1. Mark Thompson, "Transformational Growth and Disruptive Change," *American Management Association*, January 24, 2018, https://playbook.amanet.org/transformational-growth-disruptive-change-drives-leaders-behavior/.

2. Bob Tipton, "9 Stages of Transformational Change," 2012, https://teamtipton.com/nine-stages-of-transformational-change/.

3. Albert Bandura, "Psychology of Human Agency," Association for Psychological Science, speech, sixteenth annual convention, 2004.

4. PEW Research, "Concerns about Human Agency, Evolution, and Survival," Artificial Intelligence and the Future of Humans, December 10, 2018, https://ww.pewresearch.org/internet/2018/12/10/artificial-intelligence-and-the-future-of-humans/.

5. Avonlie Wilson and Julie A. Chesley, "The Benefits of Mindfulness in Leaning Transformation of Change," *Graziado Business Review*, Pepperdine University, April 6, 2016.

6. "Will Artificial Intelligence Enhance or Act Humanity?," *Wired Magazine*, April 28, 2009, https://www.wired.com/story/will-artificial-intelligence-enhance-hack-humanity/.

Epilogue
Wisdom: Mind and Heart

Imagination is more important than knowledge. For knowledge is limited, whereas imagination embraces the entire world, stimulating progress, giving birth to evolution.

—Albert Einstein

Technology is a useful servant but a dangerous master.

—Christian Lous Lange, Historian

Wisdom involves developing a set of values to think critically, creatively, and rationally, all of which are essential to achieve "good" ends. Wise individuals comprehend how positive ideas can produce negative ends. What truly matters are the ends to which knowledge is applied. Wise people use knowledge to create a better world. Action should be based on knowledge, experience, and understanding, which require ethical, academic, and moral judgment.

Technology is not evil, but it is also not blindly virtuous. Many tools can be used for either good or evil purposes. The same is true for technology. Each individual must shape his or her life and find meaning. Technology is a tool that serves people, not vice versa. But it is a tool that has no link to virtue or ethics.

Education is enamored with data. That's the big thing: collect statistical data from tests and other observations, analyze it, and come to conclusions about what is best. Sounds so easy. So scientific!

But does this data focus cause us to miss the mark? There are some things that are immeasurable. They cannot be gauged accurately through checkpoints, surveys, observables, or tests. They are too subtle and far too deep for simple metrics and data analysis.

They are things that affect the human soul and spirit and matters of the heart. They play themselves out in different ways, and in some cases, cannot be seen because they are unsaid and housed in people's feelings, perspectives, and sensitivities. They affect behavior, attitudes, relationships, and self-concept.

Expressing love or feelings is beyond algorithmic direction. Human connection is far more than analytics and it rests on feelings, some of which are discerned through intangibles and intuition. Is it possible to write algorithms to express emotional care or real emotional understanding? Human beings express love, at times, without verbally stating so. A touch on the hand says it all. People also express their feelings and emotions in different and individualistic ways.

Hearts and souls form the basis for love and emotion. Machines cannot be programmed to love. Can people fall in love, in a real sense, with machines or robots? Can he find understanding? The feelings behind words and the simple understanding and feelings that emanate when two people look at each other cannot come from artificial intelligence.

The human feeling between two people who share love is far greater than cognitive analysis or predefined phrases. Special emotional recollections are the province of human beings who can tie past experiences, even trivial ones, to deep heartfelt emotions. In the movie *Saving Private Ryan*, Captain Miller tells Private Ryan who had trouble recollecting what his brothers looked like to "think back to something specific" from the past.

He said, "Well, when I think of home, I . . . I think of something specific. I think of my, my hammock in the backyard or my wife pruning the rosebushes in a pair of my old work gloves." Something as simple as old work gloves brings back images of his wife and home, complete with warm emotion.

The heart speaks with more than words—the warmth of a simple touch, eyes connecting and communicating care and affection, the energy and warmth of one's presence, and the ability to be who one is and be accepted for the person one is. Artificial intelligence is inept at recalling special moments and times. For many, Captain Miller's memory of simple and inconsequential things brings back a tide of feeling and desire for a place called home and its relationships.

People need people, friends, coworkers, neighbors, and family to live a life of happiness and meaning. Human connection is powerful and necessary in life far more than an Internet connection. In fact, it may be the latter that stifles true relationships with other individuals because of addiction to technology and a distorted sense of being "connected."

What some fail to realize is that human intelligence, however, is more complex than artificial intelligence. The brain moves far beyond activities like respiration and digestion. Human beings can function at high levels, beyond what artificial intelligence can do.

While artificial intelligence is absent of emotional feelings, human beings, at times, act on serendipity, insight, and spirit that is totally unknown to AI. The lack of values and empathy can be disastrous because without ethical reasoning, decisions and actions can be destructive. Artificial intelligence often is totally unaware of the long-term implications of decisions and actions and their subtle ramifications.

Technology does not have emotion. The systematic cognitive approach to resolving issues or problems does not have the ability to interpret emotional or other immeasurable issues that have a dramatic effect beyond the logical plan or process. Emotional intelligence is not present because emotions are not always raised logically or by prescription. In addition, some emotions are subtle or reflected only in physical reaction.

Humans must assess the consequences of decisions and change. They must understand the impact of how things unfolded, and what forces made them better or worse. Intangibles, far beyond logical and metrically driven solutions, affect both the downsides and upsides of issues.

AI research[1] and developmental robotics is examining robots that have more complex senses: vision, audio, and touch, as well as internal information (battery level, system meeting, balance, and energy for completing tasks). Some neuroscientists believe that AI can re-create the human brain.

Human beings have bodies, senses, and cognition. Perception, history, and emotions are integral aspects of people's behavior and inclinations. Love is not based on logic. Passion, trust, intimacy, and caring are involved, all of which do not follow a recipe or algorithm. Caring, attachment, and intimacy cannot be created through a step-by-step strategic plan. Presence is more than physical, it concerns the person's total being.

Friendship and passionate love are forms of deep affection. Are they logical relationships or are there other things between people that allow them to be vulnerable, forgiving, caring, and reciprocating? True love and connectedness are beyond the scope of rational logic. Connection through love are beyond plans. It is unpredictable and unconditional. Agape is the Greek word for unconditional, divine love. Commitment and bonding with other persons—children, family, or lovers—keeps them forever connected in life and death.

AI AND LOVE

The pursuit of happiness and citizenship are two areas that people encounter throughout their lives. These two actually move beyond "wants" to the issue of needs. Just collecting material goods does not bring happiness or satisfaction. Desires may not always lead to satisfaction or purpose. For some, it takes almost a lifetime to see desires as not being purposeful and fulfilling.

Some individuals feel they have to become wealthy, but realize that it does not buy fulfillment or contentment. Parents frequently say, "I want my children to have a good life." Certainly people need health, nourishment, and social dignity. Included along with these are liberty and civil peace. Equality and dignity as human beings are essential as well as the personal connections of friends, family, and other loved ones.

Love is transformational. Its intangible nature and heartfelt impact require and generates the emotion of loving and being loved. Finding love cannot be designed on a flowchart, and certainly technology does not have a heart that can define one's true love. Emotions speak more loudly at times than data and strategic planning. Taking a life may be the moral thing to do under some rare circumstances. Will technology know when to make such an exception to an important principle? Some actions can have both positive and negative effects and interpretations. Sending someone flowers or a note, "Lovely thing you did!" can be mockery, sarcasm, or true affection.

Logic does not always work in creating the spirit and the emotional connection found in love. The heart is a physiological organ, but heartfelt love is a more complex feeling that includes physical, emotional, and indefinable attraction and connection.

Emotion stirs the heart and soul through the passionate and sentimental bonds and understanding between individuals. Can a computer code really create love between people and the continued growth and deepening of that bond? Can artificial intelligence create loving relationships? Should algorithmic logic determine one's life and depth of love for another? Love can be expressed verbally and physically, but technology cannot independently create it.

Families are often keys to a person's outlook and demeanor: human beings cannot learn about the deep aspects of life without other human beings. Passion and energy emanate from people committed to ideas and possibilities intellectually and emotionally. Passion and fervor come from deeper places than what is popular and accepted.

Feelings are not always based on reason. In fact, some people indicate the rational mind was telling them one thing, but their heart and emotions were expressing another. Life is complex and complicated. Human beings are far beyond algorithmic capability. The mind is more than the brain, it includes: thoughts and feelings, reason, and consciousness through combinations of perception, memory, emotion, will, and imagination.

NOTE

1. "Will Artificial Intelligence Ever Have Emotions or Feelings," https//www.bitbrain.com/blog/artificial-intelligence-emotions.

Bibliography

BOOKS

Adler, Mortimer J. *How to Speak—How to Listen*. New York: Touchstone, 1997.
———. *Ten Philosophical Mistakes*. New York: Touchstone, 1997.
Baker, Chris. *Artificial Intelligence—A Modern Approach*. Kindle edition, 2019.
Baumeister, Roy F. *Meaning of Life*. New York: The Guilford Press, 1991.
Bickford, Susan. *Dissonance of Democracy*. New York: Cornell University Press, 1996.
Bohm, David. *On Dialogue*. Taylor and Francis, 2012.
———. *Thought as a System*. Taylor and Francis, 2004.
Burns, James MacGregor. *Transforming Leadership*. New York: Atlantic Buckley Press, 2003.
Coeckelberg, Mark. *AI Ethics*. Cambridge, MA: The MIT Press, 2020.
Cousins, Norman. *Human Options*. New York: W. W. Norton and Company, 1981.
Dobson, Andrew. *Listening for Democracy*. Oxford: Oxford University Press, 2014.
Dweck, Carol S. *Mindset*. New York: Ballantine Books, 2008.
Ellinor, Linda, and Glenna Gerard. *Dialogue: Rediscover the Transforming Power of Conversation*. Crossroad Press, 2014.
Frankl, Viktor. *Man's Search for Meaning*. Boston: Beacon Press, 1992.
Fromm, Erich. *The Art of Listening*. Open Road Media, 2013.
Gardner, John. *Five Minds for the Future*. Boston, MA: Harvard Business Press, 2008.
———. *Frames of Mind*. New York: Basic Books, 1985.
Goens, George A. *Civility Lost: The Media, Politics, and Education*. Lanham, MD: Rowman and Littlefield, 2019.
———. *The Fog of Reform*. Lanham, MD: Rowman and Littlefield, 2016.
———. *Getting the Message*. Lanham, MD: Rowman and Littlefield, 2021.

————. *Soft Leadership for Hard Times*. Lanham, MD: Rowman and Littlefield, 2005.

Iansiti, Marco, and Karim R. Lakhani. *Competing in the Age of AI*. Over Review Press, 2020.

Isaacs, William. *Dialogue and the Art of Thinking Together*. New York: Currency Publishers, 1999.

Jacoby, Susan. *The Age of American Unreason*. New York: Vintage Books, 2009.

Johannsen, Richard L., Kathleen S. Valde, and Karen E. Whedbee. *Ethics in Human Communication*. Waveland Press, Inc., 2007.

Kahane, Adam. *Collaborating with the Enemy: How to Work with People You Don't Agree with or Like or Trust*. San Francisco: Berrett-Koehler Publishers, 2017.

Kelleher, John D. *Deep Learning*. Cambridge, MA: The MIT Press, 2019.

Laszlo, Irvine. *Macroshift: Navigating the Transformation to a Sustainable World*. San Francisco: Berrett-Koehler Publishers, 2001.

Lipari, Lisbeth. *Listening, Thinking, Being*. University Park, PA: Pennsylvania State University Press, 2014.

McGuire, Brian. *The History of Artificial Intelligence*. University of Washington, December, 2006.

Mintzberg, Henry. *The Rise and Fall of Strategic Planning*. New York: The Free Press, 1994.

Mitchell, Melanie. *Artificial Intelligence: A Guide for Thinking Humans*. New York: Farrar, Straus, and Giroux, 2019. Kindle edition.

Moldoveanu, Mihnea, and Martin, Roger Martin. *Diaminds: Decoding the Mental Habits of Successful Thinkers*. Toronto: University of Toronto Press, 2010.

National Academic Press. "Mastering a New Role: Shaping Technology Policy for National Economic Performance." 1993.

O'Donohue, John. *Eternal Echoes*. New York: Cliff Street Books, 1999.

Postman, Neil. *Technopoly*. New York: Vintage Keflex, 1993.

Rogers, Carl R., and Richard E. Farson. *Active Listening*. Mansfield Centre, CT: Martino Publishing, 2015.

Rosenberg, Nathan. "Uncertainty in Technological Change." In *The Mosaic of Economic Growth*. Stanford University Press, 1996.

Rouhiornen, Lasse. "Artificial Intelligence: 101 Things You Must No Today about Our Future." Kindle edition, 2018.

Scharmer, Otto. *Theory U: Leading from the Future as it Emerges*. San Francisco: Berret-Koehler Publishers, 2009.

Scharmer, Otto, and Katrin Kaufer. *Leading from the Emerging Future: From Ego-System to Eco-System Economies*. San Francisco: Berrett-Koehler Publishers, 2013.

Schein, Edgar H. *Humble Inquiry: The Gentle Art of Asking Instead of Telling*. San Francisco: Berrett-Koehler Publishers, 2013.

Schwartz, Peter. *The Art of the Long View*. New York: Doubleday, 1996.

Seligman, Martin E. P. *Flourish: A Visionary New Understanding of Happiness and Well-being*. Atria Books, 2011. Kindle edition.

Senge, Peter M., et al. *The Dance of Change*. New York: Currency Doubleday, 1999.

———. *Presence: And Exploration of Profound Change in People, Organizations, and Society.* The Crown Publishing Group, 2005.

Sternberg, Robert J. *Wisdom: Its Nature, Origins, and Development.* New York: Cambridge University Press, 1990.

Whyte, David. *Consolations: The Solace, Nourishment and Underlying Meaning of Every Day Words.* Langley: Many Rivers Press, 2015.

———. *The Heart Aroused.* New York: Currency Doubleday, 1994.

PERIODICALS, BLOGS, REPORTS

Anthony, Scott, Alasdair Trotter, and Evan I. Schwartz. "The 20 Top Business Transformations of the Last Decade." *Harvard Business Review*, September 24, 2019.

Ashkenas, Ron. "We Still Don't Know the Difference between Change and Transformation." *Harvard Business Review*, January 2005.

Bandura, Albert. "Psychology of Human Agency." Association for Psychological Science, speech, sixteenth annual convention, 2004.

Belden, John. "Exploring the 'Unknown Unknowns' in IT." *CIO*, December 14, 2018.

Bergstein, Brian. "What AI Still Can't Do." *Technology Review*, February 19, 2020. https://www.technologyreview.com/2020/02/19/868178/what-ai-still-cant-do/.

Brodie, Graham D. "Issues in the Measurement of Listening." *Communication Research Reports* 30. no. 1 (January–March 2013).

Brooks, David. "When Trolls and Crybullies Rule the Earth." *New Times*, May 5, 2019.

Casondra, Devine, and William L. Sparks. "Defining Moments: Toward a Comprehensive Theory of Personal Transformation." *International Journal of Humanities and Social Science* 5, no. 5 (March 2014).

Chaudron, Marcel. "Change vs. Transformation." https://rocknchange.com/change-vs-transformation/.

Davenport, Thomas, and Rajeev Ronanki. "AI for the Real World." *Harvard Business Review*, January–February 2008.

Dovere, Edward-Isaac. "The Pull of Andrew Yang's Pessimism." *The Atlantic*, August 15, 2019.

Drucker, Peter J. "The Age of Social Transformation." *Atlantic*, December 1995.

Elder, Linda. "Become a Critical Thinker." The head of the Foundation for Critical Thinking. Interview by Karen Christensen: *The Necessary Revolution in the Way We Think.* http://www.forbesindia.com/interview/rotman/become-a-critical-thinker/26592/1.

The Ethics Centre. "Ethics Explainer: Freedom of Speech." February 22, 2017. https://ethics.org.au/ethics-explainer-freedom-of-speech/.

Farwell, Drew. "Colleges Are Turning Students' Phones into Surveillance Machines, Tracking the Locations of Hundreds of Thousands." *Washington Post*, December 24, 2019. https://www.washingtonpost.com/technology/2019/12/24/

colleges-are-turning-students-phones-into-surveillance-machines-tracking-locations-hundreds-thousands/.

Fellows, James. "The 50 Greatest Breakthroughs since the Wheel." *The Atlantic*, November 2013.

The Fire. "Hate Speech." March 29, 2019. https://thefire.org/issues/hate-speech/.

Fontaine, Tim, Brian McCarthy, and Tamin Saleh. "Building the AI-Powered Organization." *Harvard Business Review*, July–August 2019.

Glessia, Silva, and Luis Carlo DiSerio. "The Sixth Wave of Innovation." *FEAUSP* 13, no. 2 (April–June 2016).

Healy, Thomas. "Whose Afraid of Free Speech?" *The Atlantic*, June 2017.

Howick Associates. "Listening Statistics." www.howickassociates.com › blog › wp-content › listening-statistics.

Huang, Ting. "Expert Systems." *The History of Artificial Intelligence*, University of Washington, 2006.

Juniu, Susana. "The Transformation of Leisure." https://www.researchgate.net/publication/261612026_The_transformation_of_leisure.

Lattier, Daniel. "Nazi Germany Was Highly Educated." https://www.intellectualtakeout.org/blog/nazi-germany-was-highly-educated/.

Mauldin, John. "The Age of Transformation." June 2014. https://www.mauldineconomics.com/frontlinethoughts/the-age-of-transformation.

McCalle, Gordon. "The Fragmentation of Culture, Learning, Teaching and Technology: Implications for the Artificial Intelligence in Educational Research Agenda in 2010." *International Journal of Artificial Intelligence in Education* (2000): 177–96.

McCarthy, John, Marvin L. Minsky, Nathaniel Rochester, and Claude E. Shannon. "A Proposal for the Dartmouth Research Project on Artificial Intelligence." *AI Magazine* 27, no. 4 (2006).

McGraven, William, James Manyika, and Adam Segal. "America Faces Fresh Challenges to Technology Innovation Leadership." *The Hill*, September 18, 2019.

McNamara, Jim. "The Lost Art of listening." Public Lecture, London School of Economics, November 23, 2016.

Minnesota State Employee Assistance Program. "Ups and Downs for Layoff Survivors." https://mn.gov/mmb/assets/ups-downs.pdf0_tcm1059-130193.pdf.

PEW Research. "Artificial Intelligence and the Future of Humans." https://www.pewresearch.org/internet/2018/12/10/artificial-intelligence-and-the-future-of-humans/.

———. "Automation in Everyday Life." https://pewresaerch.org.intenet/2017/10/04/automation.

———. "Changes in the American Workplace." https://www.pewsocialtrends.org/2016/10/06/1-changes-in-the-american-workplace/.

———. "Concerns about Human Agency, Evolution, and Survival." Artificial Intelligence and the Future of Humans, December 10, 2018. https://www.pewresearch.org/internet/2018/12/10/artificial-intelligence-and-the-future-of-humans/.

———. "How Americans See Automation and the Workplace." https://www.pewresearch.org/fact-tank/2019/04/08/how-americans-see-automation-and-the-workplace-in-7-charts/.

———. "Looking Ahead to 2050, Americans Are Pessimistic about Many Aspects of Life in US." https://www.pewresearch.org/fact-tank/2019/03/21/looking-ahead-to-2050-americans-are-pessimistic-about-many-aspects-of-life-in-u-s/.

———. "Public Predictions for the Future and Workforce Automation." https://www.pewresearch.org/internet/2016/03/10/public-predictions-for-the-future-of-workforce-automation/.

———. "7 Things We've Learned about Computer Algorithms." https://www.pewresearch.org/fact-tank/2019/02/13/7-things-weve-learned-about-computer-algorithms/.

———. "The State of American Jobs." https://pewsocialtrends.org/2016/10/06/the-state-of-American-jobs.

———. "What Americans Expect the Future of Automation to Look Like." https://www.pewresearch.org/fact-tank/2017/11/16/what-americans-expect-the-future-of-automation-to-look-like/.

Popova, Maria. "Albert Camus on Consciousness and the Lacuna Between Truth and Meaning." *Brain Pickings*, December 26, 2016.

Prysbylski, Andrew K., and Netta Weinstein. "Can You Connect with Me Now? How the Presence of Mobile Communication Technology Influences Face-to-Face Conversation Quality." *Journal of Social and Personal Relationships*, July 19, 2012.

Publishing Services-University of Minnesota Libraries. "Business Communication for Success." 2015.

RAND Corporation. "The Future of Work—Trends and Implications." https://www.rand.org/pubs/research_briefs/RB5070.html.

Rosenbush, Stephen. "Facebook's AI Chief Pushes the Technologies Limits." *Wall Street Journal*, August 13, 2020.

Ruchti, Alexander. "The Ups and Downs of Artificial Intelligence." September 15, 2019. https://www.juliusbaer.com/en/insights/artificial-intelligence/the-ups-and-downs-of-artificial-intelligence/.

Ruhl, Charlotte. "Intelligence: Definition, Theories, and Testing." *Simply Psychology*, July 16, 2020. https://www.simplypsychology.org/intelligence.html.

Samuelson, Robert J. "How 'Long Economic Waves' Could Save Capitalism." *The Washington Post*, June 14, 2020.

SAS. "Five AI Technologies That You Need to Know." https://www.sas.com/en_us/insights/articles/analytics/five-ai-technologies.html.

Schein, Edgar. H. "Dialogue, Culture, and Organizational Learning." *Reflections* 4, no. 4.

Sledzik, Karol. "Schumpeter's You and Innovation and Entrepreneurship." *SSRN Electronic Journal*, April 2013.

Stanford Medicine, Scope. "Can Artificial Intelligence Help Doctors with the Human Side of Medicine." https://scopeblog.stanford.edu/2018/12/12/can-artificial-intelligence-help-doctors-with-the-human-side-of-medicine/.

Supreme Court Justice John Paul Stevens, Speech. "The Freedom of Speech" *Yale Law School*, October 27, 1992.

Thompson, Mark. "Transformational Growth and Disruptive Change." American Management Association, January 24, 2018. https://playbook.amanet.org/transformational-growth-disruptive-change-drives-leaders-behavior/.

Tipton, Bob. "9 Stages of Transformational Change." 2012. https://teamtipton.com/nine-stages-of-transformational-change/.

Twenge, Jean M. "Have Smartphones Destroyed a Generation?" *The Atlantic*, September 2017.

United States Supreme Court. Snyder v. Philips et al. October Term, 2010. https://www.supremecourt.gov/opinions/10pdf/09-751.pdf.

Vernon, Jamie L. "Understanding the Butterfly Effect." *American Scientists* 105, no. 3 (May–June 2017).

Washington, Denzel. University of Pennsylvania Commencement Ceremony, May 16, 2011.

Wermiel, Stephen. "The Ongoing Challenge to Define Free Speech." *American Bar Association.*

"Will Artificial Intelligence Enhance or Hack Humanity." *Wire Magazine*, April 28, 2009. https://www.wired.com/story/will-artificial-intelligence-enhance-hack-humanity/.

"Will Artificial Intelligence Ever Have Emotions or Feelings." https//www.bitbrain.com/blog/artificial-intelligence-emotions.

Wilson, Avonlie, and Julie A. Chesley. "The Benefits of Mindfulness in Leaning Transformation of Change." *Graziado Business Review*, Pepperdine University, April 6, 2016.

Index

Adler, Mortimer, 89
age of capitalism, 82
algorithm, 46, 48, 60, 67–69, 72,
    74–75, 82–85
AlphaGo, 62, 82
American Civil Liberties Union, 57, 75
American Dream, 90
artificial intelligence, 44–47;
    artificial general intelligence, 46–47;
    artificial narrow intelligence, 46;
    artificial super intelligence, 47;
    downside, 24;
    feelings, 97–98, 104–5
Asimov, Isaac, 74

Bandura, Albert, 96
Belden, John, 54–55;
    knowns and unknowns, 54–55, 103
Bell, Alexander Graham, 33
biases, 18, 52, 69
Black Swan, 51
bureaucracy, 6
Butterfly Effect, 3, 51

calling, 19, 27, 94
causal reasoning, 76
chaos, 1, 11, 15–17, 23
chatbots, 62
cognitive engagement, 46;

insight, 62;
    intelligence, 43;
    skills, 48, 81, 85
courage, 19, 29
COVID-19, 35
creative destruction, 36
creativity, 2, 14, 25, 42, 47, 61, 73,
    79–80, 85–86, 98–99, 101

Danish oil and gas:
    OSted, 10
Deep Blue, 45
defining moments, 40, 90–91
dialogue, 40, 90–91
Drucker, Peter, 35

education, 87–91, 100
education vs. schooling, 80–82, 89–90
emotional intelligence, 10
emotional understanding, 97–98, 104
employment, 7–8, 16, 20, 28, 33, 36,
    53, 71, 100;
    job loss, 83
ethics, 22;
    and innovation, 83–84;
    and thinking, 85–87, 91

failure, 4, 17, 52, 62, 80
feelings, 38, 64, 85, 95

About the Author

George A. Goens, PhD, has written seven books and coauthored four others on leadership, school reform, education, and social issues. He served as an executive in teaching positions, as well as leadership consultant to public boards and individuals.